Freedom from Mithraism

Overcoming the False Verdicts of Mithraism

by

Dr. Ron M. Horner

Freedom from Mithraism

Overcoming the False Verdicts of Mithraism

By

Dr. Ron M. Horner

www.CourtsOfHeaven.Net
PO Box 2167
Albemarle, North Carolina 28002

Freedom from Mithraism

Overcoming the False Verdicts of Mithraism

Copyright © 2020 Dr. Ron M. Horner

Scripture is taken from the New King James Version®. Copyright © 1982 by Thomas Nelson. Used by permission. All rights reserved. (Unless otherwise noted.)

Scripture quotations marked (AMP) are taken from the Amplified® Bible (AMP), Copyright © 1954, 1958, 1962, 1964, 1965, 1987 by The Lockman Foundation.

Scripture quotations marked (TPT) are taken from The Passion Translation®. Copyright © 2017 by BroadStreet Publishing® Group, LLC. Used by permission. All rights reserved.

All rights reserved. This book is protected by the copyright laws of the United States of America. This book may not be copied or reprinted for commercial gain or profit. The use of short quotations or occasional page copying for personal or group study is permitted and encouraged. Permission will be granted upon request.

Any trademarks or service marks used are the property of their respective owners.

Requests for bulk sales discounts, editorial permissions, or other information should be addressed to:

LifeSpring Publishing
PO Box 2167
Albemarle, NC 28002 USA
www.lifespringpublishing.com

Additional copies available at www.courtsofheaven.net

ISBN 13 TP: 978-1-953684-04-2
ISBN 13 eBook: 978-1-953684-05-9

Cover Design by Darian Horner Design (www.darianhorner.com)
Image: stock.adobe.com: #129012466, #217324846, 123rf.com: #85834117

First Edition: December 2020

10 9 8 7 6 5 4 3 2 1

Printed in the United States of America

Table of Contents

Acknowledgements i

Preface iii

Chapter 1 What Do We Know? 1

Chapter 2 Setting the Stage 7

Chapter 3 First Degree
Corax – the Raven 17

Chapter 4 Second Degree
Nymphus, the Male Bride 29

Chapter 5 Third Degree
Miles, the Soldier 39

Chapter 6 Fourth Degree
Leo, the Lion 47

Chapter 7 Fifth Degree
Peres/Perseus, the Persian 57

Chapter 8 Sixth Degree
Heliodromus, the Sun Runner 65

Chapter 9 Seventh Degree
Pater, the Father 73

Chapter 10 Closing Prayer 83

Chapter 11 Final Instructions 87

Chapter 12 The Court of Reclamations 91

Chapter 13 Plundering the Enemies Camp.. 97

Chapter 14 Conclusion 103

Works Cited... 109

Appendix A 111

A Short Explanation of Lingering Human Spirits............................ 111

A Testimony.. 115

Description... 117

About the Author 119

Other Books by Dr. Ron M. Horner.. 121

Acknowledgements

Several people assisted with the origins and development of this book. First, my thanks go to Kay Tolman who has pioneered the understanding of the bondages created through Mithraism for many years in her ministry. She gave me my first real understanding of the Cult of Mithras. Thank you, Kay.

Next, I want to thank my CourtsNet Class of 2020 for their work in determining the many false verdicts of Mithraism and for allowing this course to "kick their butt". Special thanks to Janine Villines and Jeremy Friedman whose contributions helped shorten the writing time for this book. Also, thanks to Fran Wipf for her editorial help. Thank you, ladies, and gentlemen.

And, as always, thanks to my lovely wife Adina.

Preface

The Body of Christ is being awakened to the extent to which paganism has been intertwined with Christianity throughout the centuries. Many traditions and teachings that we accept as part of Christianity have, upon closer examination, been borrowed from ancient pagan religions. These spiritual connections to pagan entities are creating unnecessary bondages in the Body of Christ.

Most believers are totally unfamiliar with Mithraism, so the impact of it on their lives, and their generations, has been able to work undetected. A simple hint as to whether Mithraism is present in the genealogy was demonstrated to me at a conference I attended in 2019. As Kay Tolman was teaching, she noted that the repeated use of certain names within your family tree may indicate historical allegiance to the false gods of Mithraism. In the audience, a lady mentioned her husband Leon, whose father was Leonard, who grandfather was another form of Leo. Scattered throughout her husbands' lineage were instances of various forms of Leo – the name of the Leontocephaline – the lion of Mithraism. Other names associated with Mithraism can be Miles and Peter in their various forms. Repeated uses of these names, throughout a family line, may have started out as a form of homage to the various associated gods; but over time, the original meaning was lost to the understanding of the family.

Many of us have ties to Mithraism on some level. As you move forward in this book, allow Holy Spirit to highlight when you have knowingly or unknowingly come into agreement with this false religion through words, oaths, covenants, rituals, traditions, or more.

Much of this book is presented in the form of courtroom scenarios that will allow you to deal with the legal ground that allows Mithraism to impact your life.

Before you begin the courtroom scenarios, simply speak to your soul, and tell it to step back and call your spirit to come forward and take its proper place in your being – that of being the driver, not the passenger. We are spirit beings who have a soul contained in a physical body. Our spirit should be the predominant factor in our life on the earth. However, most of us have never learned this concept, and our souls dominate by default. By living spirit first and bypassing your soul, you can attain the healing and freedom that your spirit is designed to impart into your life.

Secondly, call your personal angels to come near and assist you as you proceed through the scenarios in this book. Instruct them to protect all your realms, gates, and bridges as you work through this process. Instruct them to evict any trespassers and to remove all spiritual debris left by the courtroom activity you are completing through this book.

Understand that you may have various experiences as you work through this book. Make a firm commitment to go all the way through. It may be necessary to give your soul a break as you go through each degree level a lot will be shifting in the spirit realm. You may sense chains breaking off your life or your lineage. If so, enjoy the freedom. You may notice your spiritual sight is opening more and more. You may even feel as if a heaviness has lifted from you. Enjoy these new levels of freedom and give praise to the Father for your newfound liberty.

Invite Holy Spirit to guide you in this journey to freedom from Mithraism. Stay sensitive to your spirit and to Holy Spirit and remain determined to finish the work in this book - however slowly you need to proceed. Remember, it will be worth it. Our prayer for you is that your eyes will be opened to truth as you work through this revelation, and that you experience tremendous freedom as a result.

Chapter 1
What Do We Know?

Mithraism is a little-known, pagan religion, thousands of years old. It has had far more impact upon our lives and culture than we even care to realize. Entire church structures have Mithraism at its foundational level, and traditions that originated in Mithraism have simply been accepted as a normal part of the church for centuries.

One of the most important historical figures in the history of the Christian church was the Emperor Constantine I. He is the one cited for bringing legitimacy to Christianity, elevating it from a sect to a dominant force on the earth. However, with a little digging you will find that there is more to the story.

> *During the 1st century BC, a cult of Mithra made much progress in Rome, after enduring persecution, when some Emperors adopted the religion... Mithra became extremely popular among the Roman legionaries and later even among the Emperors. The worship of Mithra was first recognized by Emperor Aurelian and he instituted the cult of "Sol Invictus" or the Invincible Sun. Emperor Diocletian also a worshipper of Mithra, the*

Sun God, burned much of the Christian scriptures in 307 A.D.

This enabled Emperor Constantine to merge the cult of Mithra with that of Christianity that was developing much. He declared himself a Christian but at the same time maintained his ties to the Mithra cult. He retained the title "Pontifus Maximus" the high priest. On his coins were inscribed: "Sol Invicto comiti" which means, committed to the invincible sun. This new blend of the two faiths, he officially proclaimed as Christianity. Christianity spread all over the Roman Empire and Eastern Europe by massive persecution and brought an end to a variety of religions that flourished there.[1]

Have we considered the impact of the fact that Constantine NEVER renounced his allegiance to Mithra and maintained his status as a priest of the Mithras cult? He may not have been the "friend of Christianity" that he has been touted as being through the centuries. He saw the political potential of incorporating the New Testament church and creating a powerful economic and social force. What he succeeded in doing was creating a mixture of the pagan with the holy in numerous ways, and of removing the apostolic model of church ministry and replacing it with the pastoral model of ministry that we are accustomed to today.

It was Constantine that designated December 25th as the recognized birth date of Jesus Christ. Coincidentally, this was also the birthdate of Mithras, the Sun God. Few biblical scholars believe that Jesus was born in December, so was this just a convenient way

---

[1] Crabtree, 2017

to overlay one celebration upon the foundations of another? Was this another attempt to induce paganize mixture into Christianity?

Jewish customs and feasts were commonly featured within Christianity at the time, and Constantine outlawed these linkages. It was also Constantine who dedicated Sunday as the "The Lord's Day" in Christianity – a day of worship and rest - with Sunday being the typical day of worship for Christians as opposed to the Jewish Sabbath which was typically observed on Saturday. Note too that name of the day of the week designated for "Christian" worship – 'Sun' day– interesting considering one of the prominent deities in Mithraism is the Sun.

Many things are attributed to Constantine that may have been good, but the mixture of the profane with the holy has cost the church dearly throughout its history. Boldly, I will say that the church lost considerable ground because of this mixture of the profane with the holy. Of particular concern is the removal of the apostolic paradigm under which the church had functioned, and its replacement with the pastoral model as a result of Constantine's actions. These details of these events I will leave with the church historians and theologians. The purpose of this book is to help you find freedom from the clutches of Mithraism that are likely a major source of the trouble you have had in your life.

This book will be patterned after my book *Overcoming the False Verdicts of Freemasonry* in its approach and method. If you have not gone through that book, I would recommend that you do so in addition to working through this book. If you have gone through the Freemasonry book, this Mithraism book is a powerful adjunct to help you gain complete freedom. Many of the foundations of Freemasonry find their roots in the Cult of Mithra. Freemasonry adopted many aspects of Mithraism.

Just as Freemasonry has affected the church, so has Mithraism. Mithraism was widely practiced at the same time that Constantine imposed Christianity, and he incorporated many Mithraic practices into the Catholicism that he was seeking to develop and promote. There are familiar parallels between the two religions including various oaths, ceremonies, degrees, and titles.

The correlation between the Seventh Degree of Mithraism - the Pater degree - and the position of the Pope is alarming. You will see this when dealing with the Seventh Degree of Mithraism in this book.

To see how the influence of Mithraism has impacted the church, consider the fact that St. Peter's Basilica in Rome is built on the original site of the Circus of Nero, also known as the Circus of Caligula, where hundreds of early saints were martyred during Nero's reign. Also, the obelisk in St. Peter's square came from the center of the Circus of Nero where it formerly stood. Additionally, a portion of the basilica complex is built on top of a pagan gravesite. Although the site was supposedly chosen because the Apostle Peter was buried there, it is hardly holy ground. Although you may have been raised in the Catholic faith these historical facts have probably never been mentioned or explained. What we thought was holy seems to have corrupted foundations. I am not bashing the Catholic faith, nor am I bashing Protestants. I simply am exposing aspects that were probably unknown to most of us. The vast majority in either camp were and are merely seeking relationship with God. We simply did not know some of the roots or foundations upon which many things were built.

When Protestants broke away from the Catholic church to develop the Protestant faith, some of these Mithraic practices were included in the new structure. Hence, the entire Christian heritage since Constantine has been impacted in one way or another by

Mithraism. When the separation from the Catholic church at the leading of Martin Luther occurred, these "protestants" did not revert to a more Book of Acts style of Christianity, they simply did away with some of the practices of the Catholic Church, practices that were the subject of Martin Luther's 95 Theses.

If you were raised outside of the vestiges of Christian religions with any sort of a New Age background, you would also have a connection to Mithraism with its worship of the sun, moon, planets, and more. If you had ancestors - or were yourself - involved in Freemasonry, then this book applies to you because the source of many of the elements of Freemasonry originated in the false religion of Mithraism.

This book will contain brief summaries of the seven degrees of Mithraism and some details about them, but it will by no means be exhaustive other resources are available elsewhere for those who wish to better understand the specifics of Mithraism. The goal of this book is your freedom from the impact of this ancient cult upon your life and family. As you progress through this book, you will be invited to pray aloud the prayers of repentance and work through the court scenarios to deal with the false verdicts of each degree level of Mithraism.

Just as in the Freemasonry book, I purport that each degree level of Mithraism has associated false verdicts that empower each degree level. Until those false verdicts are overturned in the Courts of Heaven, true freedom cannot be realized because each verdict has a legal right to impact your life until it is dealt with in the courts. Work through each degree level slowly and methodically. Be sensitive to Holy Spirit to the instructions and hints He may give concerning the ways in which your life has been impacted. Sensitivity is key in this process, as is repentance. We have found in our years of working in the Courts of Heaven that the more repentant we are, the more we are accomplish within the Courts of Heaven.

In summary, any of the following may indicate that your family line has some connection to Mithraism, and you are likely to benefit from the concepts in this book:

- Do you have Freemasonry in your ancestry?
- Do you have trouble seeing spiritually?
- Do you find instances of repeated family names along the lines of Leon, Miles, and Peter in your family tree?
- Do you find a fascination with the stars, moon, or sun prevalent in your family tree?
- Have you, or any of your ancestors, participated in organized religion, or any pagan practices?

If you answered yes to any of these questions, this book will help you begin to unravel yourself from the impacts of Mithraism in your life.

If you answered no to the above, I challenge you to work through this book anyway. You will likely be surprised at what is uncovered.

Chapter 2
Setting the Stage

As you begin this process of freedom from Mithraism, you will want to set the stage for full participation by yourself and your cloud of witnesses. Speak to your soul to back up. Call your spirit to come forward and be the dominant voice while you go through these prayers and courtroom scenarios. Your soul will likely be resistant to the courtroom scenarios, so you need to set your will to complete the task ahead of you.

Call your angel(s) to come near to assist you. Invite the hosts of Heaven to assist you, and to direct your path, and give you counsel today.

Now, request access to the Court of Cancellations within the Courts of Heaven. The following petition is for the releasing of yourself and your bloodline generations from the profane worship of Mithras. As you go through this petition you may not understand all that is being requested, but it gives clues as to the various bondages to which you may have been subjected.

As you work through this book, you will be performing identificational repentance on behalf of your own deeds, as well as those of your ancestors (living or dead). In doing so, you are accepting that because you are their ancestor, you have become a legal recipient of any covenants, agreements, or oaths they may have made - just as you would be the legal recipient of certain agreements that your mother or father may have made.

As you pray through this book, you will need to recite aloud each courtroom scenario. Wherever you see the headings: Courtroom Scenario, False Verdicts, Repentance, Forgiveness, Requests, Conclusion, and Further Instruction, you will need to verbally recite what is written. At the end of each chapter is an encouragement for awaiting further instructions from Heaven. Do not rush through the book. Let Holy Spirit have time to work in your heart.

Begin with the following:

Courtroom Scenario

Your Honor, I request access to the Court of Cancellations today, in Jesus' name. I petition this Court, requesting a verdict that grants freedom to me, and my generational bloodlines, from the acts of profane worship of Mithras, engaged in by me and/or my bloodline ancestors, all the way back to the hand of the Father, and all the way forward as far as it needs to go.

Repentance

Just Judge, I repent for all engagement with Mithraism by myself or my generations. I ask this Court to hear my repentance as I confess Mithraism as sin against God.

I confess as sin and repent for all participation in Mithras rituals and participation in Mithras orders throughout my family line.

I repent for all participation in the initiation rites and purification rites of Mithraism.

I repent for all profane worship of all principalities and powers associated with Mithraism and all dedications to this false religion.

I repent for my participation and/or the participation of any of my ancestors in the false catechism and false gospel of Mithraism.

I repent for the giving over of our lives and generations to Mithras.

I repent for accepting the blood of a bull as a key to my salvation.

I repent for the worship of the Lion of Mithraism.

I repent for those in my generations who perpetuated this false religion in my family line, in Jesus' name.

I repent for every allegiance to Mithras on any level, at any time, in any place, realm, or dimension by me or my generations.

I repent for every secret password and handshake used in Mithraic orders.

I repent for worship of the false god Mithras as the angel of light.

I repent for the worship of the sun, moon, stars, planets, and constellations.

I repent for embracing the lies of Mithraism by me and my generations.

I repent for embracing the false religion of Mithraism in whatever form, and by whatever name, it was represented to me or my generations.

I repent for all engagement in witchcraft in any form, on any level, and in any dimension, in Jesus' name.

I repent for embracing hypnotism.

I repent for embracing the Tauroctony[2] and all its occult meaning.

I repent for the defilement of our lives and generations by participating in the rituals and practices of Mithraism and for engaging in activities in Mithraic temples.

I repent for participating in guided visualization associated with Mithraism.

I repent for the shapeshifting involved in Mithraism.

I repent for all participation in magic and shamanism.

I repent for all financial support of Mithraism in any fashion.

I repent for the embrace of:

> The seven heavens and seven heavenly gates of Mithraism
>
> The seven rungs of the ladder
>
> The seven metals and seven planets
>
> The false torch and the false sword

---

[2] Tauroctony are the stone reliefs depicting the killing of a bull central to the cult of Mithraism. *Tauroctonos* means "bull killing".

I repent for the singing of hymns or songs to Mithras.

I repent for all evangelism of this false religion and for the entrapping of others in these false beliefs.

I repent for the use of and participation with Tarot cards and all divination.

I repent for participating in the qualifying ordeals of Mithraism:

> Fire
>
> Heat
>
> Cold
>
> Hunger
>
> Thirst

I repent for everyone in my generations who embraced the false knowings of Mithraism.

I repent for worship of the many Egyptian gods and idols.

I repent for placing other gods before you, Lord of Hosts.

I repent for participating in the Magical Dinner and for partaking of false communions.

I repent for the kissing of the amulets in the liturgy of Mithraism and for the exchange of DNA in homage to these false gods.

I repent for participation in the liturgy of the Mithraic mass.

I repent for chanting according to the liturgy of Mithraism.

I repent for every trade with the false gods of Mithraism and for utilizing the benefits of these trades by me or my ancestors.

I repent for all these acts and actions committed by me or by my generations.

I hereby surrender to Jesus every title, office, authority, or delegation related to Mithraism that I, or my bloodline ancestors, obtained through profane worship of Mithras.

* * * * *

You also may be impressed to go further with your repentance. Follow Holy Spirit's leading here and as you go through the remaining courtroom scenarios related to Mithraism.

Forgiveness

I forgive those human agents of darkness who devised and formulated this false religion without regard for, or despite, Your holy commandments. I forgive, bless, and release them in Jesus name. I forgive as I have been forgiven.

I forgive every ancestor who tied me to the covenants of Mithraism at any and every level, at any time, in any dimension. I release them this day from their guilt.

I ask forgiveness for any actions that introduced trauma into me and my bloodlines.

I ask that the trauma and fear be removed, in Jesus' name.

I forgive these ancestors for introducing this wickedness into my bloodline and I also forgive those who perpetuated it throughout the generations.

I forgive, bless, and release each of these persons, in Jesus' name.

Requests

I request, in the Courts of Heaven today, a complete severing of all ownership claims, titles, agreements, oaths, contracts or covenants, including blood covenants, made by me or my ancestors at any time, in any place, realm, or dimension.

I request the cancellation of every contract, agreement, and oath with Mithras, Helios, Saturn, Ahura Mazda, the Saturnalia Brotherhood, and any other principality or power by whatever name, in the name of Jesus Christ.

I ask that all ownership claims be cancelled and entirely severed from my life and my generations, including all claims of ownership of my seed or the seed of my generations.

I request an absolute divorce from Baal, Mithras, and every false deity associated with this pagan religion and profane worship.

I request the severing of the power of pharmakeia off me and my generations and repent for everyone who embraced the false knowings of Mithraism.

I request, in lieu of the covenants of death and the agreements with Sheol made through the false worship of Mithraism, that those covenants of death be entirely annulled, and that instead, a covenant of life be issued to me through the blood and body of Jesus Christ, as my Messiah and Redeemer.

I request Permanent Cease and Desist Orders from astral projection, silver cord entwining, and all other access and activities of the ungodly entities associated with Mithraism.

I request the cancellation of every curse, spell, hex, vex, hinx, jinx, incantation, voodoo, sorcery, form of witchcraft, dark art, enchantment, smote, or any other activity affecting me or any of my generations via allegiances to the false gods of Mithraism.

I request the cancellation of every curse spoken over my ancestors and/or their generations in funeral rituals or at any other time, in Jesus' name.

I request the removal and obliteration of all satanic seals and records, pertaining to me or my family line, from the courts of hell regarding each ceremony of Mithraism in all its forms.

I request the complete evacuation from my life, and from my generations, of every ungodly entity in Jesus' name. I request that these entities be captured, put in chains, and escorted or sent directly to the feet of Jesus.

Conclusion

Today, I stand as a representative of my bloodline in Your Court. I request that the repentance for my bloodline be recorded in all pertinent courts, be used in other pertinent court cases, and be recorded in the books of Heaven for me and for my generations. I also request the immediate release of the Lord's blessings that have been held back or lost to me and my generations because of connections to Mithraism.

I thank you Just Judge and this court for hearing my repentance and requests this day and I request these things today in the Courts of Heaven, in Jesus' name.

Prayed this ____ day of _____, _____.

By _____

Further Instructions

Now, as you await the verdict, listen carefully for any further instructions you may be given. Once a favorable verdict is rendered, you will sense a flood of peace into your being. You may also experience other manifestations as the formerly attached entities make their exit from your life. Rejoice with gratitude for the new level of freedom you will now experience!

As a prophetic act, remove the symbolic marriage ring and give it to the angel attending you. Also, remove any regalia[3] associated with this degree, handing it to the angel for disposal.

You also may be impressed to go further with your repentance. Follow Holy Spirit's leading here and as you go through the remaining courtroom scenarios related to Mithraism.

---

[3] Regalia – special garments worn in ceremonial situations. May include special jewelry or headgear.

Chapter 3
First Degree

Corax – the Raven

Each degree of Mithraism has certain specifics associated with that degree. At the time of this pagan religion, only seven planets were known to exist. That is why Mithraism contains seven distinct degree levels. Each degree level was a dedication to one or more of the planets, as well as to the sun or moon, or both.

Worship of the sun god is typically known as Baal, while the moon god is Allah. In the appendix of my book, *Overcoming the False Verdicts of Freemasonry*, you will find each of these prayers: The Divorce from Baal and The Divorce from the Moon God. If you have not yet worked through those two petitions, I recommend that you do so.

In the First Degree of Mithraism, known as the Corax (the Raven) degree, one is placed under the protection of the planet Mercury. The false god worshipped is Hermes – the messenger of the gods. The ritual symbol was the beaker and caduceus, and the symbolism was the death of the neophyte. The raven has some correlation to the foul bird mentioned in Revelation 18:2 which is an entity of darkness that has been little known to the church. I discuss this creature in my book *Engaging Heaven for Revelation*.

Courtroom Scenario

In Jesus' name, I request access to the Appeals Court of Heaven.

Just Judge, I stand here on behalf of myself [state your full name] and on behalf of my bloodlines – past, present, and future – everyone related to me by blood, marriage, adoption, civil or religious covenant.

I also ask that my cloud of witnesses be allowed to be present in the courtroom today.

False Verdicts

I ask that the false verdicts entered into at the Corax or Raven degree (First Degree) be overturned and replaced with righteous verdicts on my behalf and on behalf of my bloodlines, in Jesus' name.

These false verdicts are as follows:

> *Birds are liaisons between heaven and earth and are messengers of the sun god Baal.*
>
> *Being identified in the Cult of Mithras is a holy thing.*
>
> *Astral travel is a holy way of travel and necessary to fulfill my duties to the gods of Mithraism.*
>
> *Mithraism provides an alternate and better way to achieve resurrection into a New Man.*

The rites, rituals, and all components of Mithraism are superior to all other religions and are foundational understandings of godhood and perfection.

Baptism into Mithraism results in my sins being forgiven.

Shape-shifting and shamanism are acceptable practices before the Lord God Jehovah.

Mithraism provides superior knowledge and wisdom – particularly about the sciences and medicine.

Repentance

I repent for the participation and initiation in the Corax, the Raven, the First Degree of Mithraism with the offices, titles, regalia, oaths, vows, and initiation rites of this degree.

I repent for receiving the title and office of "Messenger of the Gods."

I repent for me and my bloodlines receiving the title and office of "Corax, the Raven."

I repent for embracing the false belief that to be identified in the Cult of Mithras is a holy thing.

I repent for participating in and accepting the titles, offices, oaths, vows, and initiation rites of the First Degree of Mithraism.

I repent for all allegiance to Mithraism and surrender all membership into Mithras Orders over to Jesus Christ.

I repent for all worship of Mercury or Hermes, in any form or fashion, and for all ungodly trades made with these false gods.

I repent for my own involvement, knowingly or unknowingly, that tied me to the covenants of Mithraism at whatever level, at any time, in any realm or dimension.

I also repent for the involvement of those in my family line that involved themselves in Mithraism, whether knowingly or unknowingly. I release them this day from their guilt and bless them.

I repent for any actions, including those of myself or others, that introduced trauma into me and my bloodlines. I ask that the trauma and fear be removed, and that every trauma bond to time be healed in Jesus' name.

I repent for embracing the false verdict declaring:

> *Birds are liaisons between heaven and earth and are messengers of the sun god Baal.*

I repent for any and all allegiances to Baal by whatever form, in any place, time, realm, or dimension in Jesus' name.

I repent for embracing this wicked bird, and its works, and for inviting them into my life and my ancestry.

I repent for embracing the false verdict declaring:

> *Astral travel is a holy way of travel and necessary to fulfill my duties to the gods of Mithraism.*

I repent for engaging in astral travel by myself and/or my bloodlines, and for embracing the false belief that to do so was a fulfillment of duties to the gods of Mithraism.

I repent for embracing the false verdict declaring:

Mithraism provides an alternate and better way to achieve resurrection into a New Man.

I repent for the rejection of the resurrection of Jesus Christ and the embrace of a false resurrection as taught by Mithraism. I recognize that I can only become a new man through Jesus Christ, and that Jesus himself is the Resurrection and the Life[4].

I repent for embracing the false verdict declaring:

> *The rites, rituals, and all components of Mithraism are superior to all other religions and are foundational understandings of godhood and perfection.*

I repent for accepting this false verdict as truth, for rejecting the knowledge of the one true God, and for accepting the false teachings of Mithraism as truth.

I repent for embracing the false verdict declaring:

> *Baptism into Mithraism results in my sins being forgiven.*

I repent for embracing the false baptism of Mithraism and of believing that such an act provides forgiveness of sins outside of the perfect sacrifice of Jesus Christ and the shedding of His blood on my behalf.

---

[4] John 11:25

I repent for embracing the false verdict declaring:

> *Shape-shifting and shamanism are acceptable practices before the Lord God Jehovah.*

I repent for engaging or permitting shape-shifting and engaging in shamanism by myself or my bloodlines. Such practices are detestable to a holy God, and I request forgiveness of these sins, in Jesus' name.

I repent for embracing the false verdict declaring:

> *Mithraism provides superior knowledge and wisdom – particularly regarding the sciences and medicine.*

I repent for the embrace of the Tree of the Knowledge of Good and Evil espoused by this false verdict and for the rejection of the Tree of Life. Only through Jesus Christ can truth and wisdom come.

I repent for embracing the false beliefs of Mithraism regarding science and medicine. You alone, Lord God, are the source of all knowledge and are the source of healing for our lives.

Please replace the false verdict stating that

> *Birds are liaisons between heaven and earth and are messengers of the sun god Baal*

with righteous verdicts, for Your Word declares in Romans 1:19-25:

> *Because what may be known of God is manifest in them (unbelievers), for God has shown it to them. [20] For since the creation of the world His invisible attributes are clearly seen, being understood by the things that are made, even His eternal power and Godhead, so that*

> they are without excuse, ²¹ because, although they knew God, they did not glorify Him as God, nor were thankful, but became futile in their thoughts, and their foolish hearts were darkened. ²² Professing to be wise, they became fools, ²³ and changed the glory of the incorruptible God into an image made like corruptible man – and birds and four-footed animals and creeping things. ²⁴ Therefore God also gave them up to uncleanness, in the lusts of their hearts, to dishonor their bodies among themselves, ²⁵ who exchanged the truth of God for the lie and worshiped and served the creature rather than the Creator, who is blessed forever. Amen. (Additions mine)

We therefore are not to worship birds or any other creatures and elevate them above your original purpose and design.

Concerning the second false verdict that astral travel is a holy way of travel and necessary to fulfill my duties to the gods of Mithraism, Your Word declares what Jesus said in Matthew 22:37-40:

> 'You shall love the Lord your God with all your heart, with all your soul, and with all your mind.' ³⁸ This is the first and great commandment. ³⁹ And the second is like it: 'You shall love your neighbor as yourself.' ⁴⁰ On these two commandments hang all the Law and the Prophets."

Regarding the false verdict stating that Mithraism provides an alternate and better way to achieve resurrection into a New Man,

Your word in Ephesians 2:13-16, says:

> But now in Christ Jesus you who once were far off have been brought near by the blood of Christ. ¹⁴ For He

> *Himself is our peace, who has made both one, and has broken down the middle wall of separation, [15] having abolished in His flesh the enmity, that is, the law of commandments contained in ordinances, to create in Himself one new man from the two, thus making peace, [16] and that He might reconcile them both to God in one body through the cross, thereby putting to death the enmity.*

Your Word also states in Joel 2:32:

> *And it shall come to pass that whoever calls on the name of the LORD Shall be saved. For in Mount Zion and in Jerusalem there shall be deliverance, As the LORD has said, Among the remnant whom the LORD calls.*

Salvation only comes through Jesus Christ, Your Son as declared in Acts 4:12:

> *Nor is there salvation in any other (besides Jesus), for there is no other name under Heaven given among men by which we must be saved." (Clarifications mine)*

Regarding the false verdict stating that the rites, rituals, and all components of Mithraism are superior to all other religions and are foundational understandings of godhood and perfection - that is in direct contradiction to Your Word, as described in Joel 2:32, Ephesians 2:13-16 and other Scriptures already mentioned.

The false verdict indicating that baptism into Mithraism results in my sins being forgiven is also in direct contradiction to the Word of God as previously outlined.

Also, the false verdicts that shape-shifting and shamanism are acceptable practices before the Lord God Jehovah. As shamanism is a form of idolatry and an ungodly practice, it also is in contradiction to the Word of God. Shape shifting is a violation of Your holy truth that we are each made in the image of God.

And finally, the false verdict of the First Degree level stating that Mithraism provides superior knowledge and wisdom – particularly regarding the sciences and medicine - contradicts your Word in John 14:6 where it states that Jesus is the way, the truth, and the life and no one can come to the Father except through Him.

*****

You also may be impressed to go further with your repentance. Following Holy Spirit's leading here and as you go through the Courtroom Scenarios related to Mithraism.

Forgiveness

I forgive those human agents of darkness who devised and formulated this false religion without regard for, or despite, Your holy commandments. I forgive, bless, and release them in Jesus name. I forgive as I have been forgiven.

I forgive every ancestor who tied me to the covenants of Mithraism at any and every level, at any time, in any dimension. I release them this day from their guilt.

I ask forgiveness for any actions that introduced trauma into me and my bloodlines.

I ask that the trauma and fear be removed, in Jesus' name.

I forgive these ancestors for introducing this wickedness into my bloodline and I also forgive those who perpetuated it throughout the generations.

I forgive, bless, and release each of these persons, in Jesus' name.

Requests

I ask that these false verdicts be overturned in the Courts of Heaven this day and replaced with righteous verdicts and that I and my bloodlines be released from every bondage resulting from my involvement in the First Degree level of Mithraism. I request that all damage to my DNA and the DNA of my lineage be healed, every spot be removed, and every blemish undone in Jesus' name.

I request that every ungodly trade be cancelled, and every form of taxation be lifted from me and my bloodlines.

I request the cancellation of every impact and ramification of the allegiances, covenants, oaths, vows, or dedications to Mithraism through this first degree in Jesus' name.

I ask that the trauma and fear be removed, and that every trauma bond to time be healed in Jesus' name.

Additionally, I request that all these actions be applied to everyone related to me by blood, marriage, adoption, civil or religious covenant, all the way back to the hand of the Father and all the way forward as far as it needs to go, in Jesus' mighty name.

Conclusion

Today, I stand as a representative of my bloodline in Your Court. I request that the repentance for my bloodline be recorded in all pertinent courts, be used in other pertinent court cases, and be recorded in the books of Heaven for me and for my generations.

I also request the immediate release of the Lord's blessings that have been held back or lost to me and my generations because of connections to Mithraism.

I thank you Just Judge and this court for hearing my repentance and requests this day and I request these things today in the Courts of Heaven, in Jesus' name.

Prayed this ____ day of _____, _____.

By _____

Further Instructions

Now, as you await the verdict, listen carefully for any further instructions you may be given. Once a favorable verdict is rendered, you will sense a flood of peace into your being. You may also experience other manifestations as the formerly attached entities make their exit from your life. Rejoice with gratitude for the new level of freedom you will now experience!

As a prophetic act, remove the symbolic marriage ring and give it to the angel attending you. Also, remove any regalia[5] associated with this degree, handing it to the angel for disposal.

You also may be impressed to go further with your repentance. Follow Holy Spirit's leading here and as you go through the remaining courtroom scenarios related to Mithraism.

---

[5] Regalia – special garments worn in ceremonial situations. May include special jewelry or headgear.

Chapter 4
Second Degree

Nymphus, the Male Bride

In this Second Degree, the Nymphus or Male Bride degree, one comes under the protection of Venus. The false gods worshipped are Mithras and Venus, and the ritual symbols are the "Veil of Reality", "Light of Truth", Chrysalis, veil, torch, mirror, bell, and diadem. The symbolism includes a false marriage, and a false resurrection.

Again, pagan worship of the created over the Creator is involved, leading one to embrace a false reality, to submit to spiritual blindness via the "veil of reality," to submit to a false light of truth, and other pagan symbolism.

Courtroom Scenario

In Jesus' name, I request access to the Appeals Court of Heaven.

Just Judge, I stand here on behalf of myself _[state your full name]_ and on behalf of my bloodlines – past, present, and future –

everyone related to me by blood, marriage, adoption, civil or religious covenant.

I also ask that my cloud of witnesses be allowed to be present in the courtroom today.

False Verdicts

I ask that the false verdicts entered into at the Nymphus or Male Bride (Second Degree) be replaced with righteous verdicts on my behalf and on behalf of my bloodlines, in Jesus' name.

These false verdicts are as follows:

> *The office of Bride of Mithras (Nymphus the bridegroom) is a sacred office with all its oaths, vows, covenants, loyalty, eternality, and fidelity of this Second Degree and is in some fashion holy.*
>
> *The offering of the cup represents my heart and water demonstrates my love to Mithras is holy.*
>
> *The bread is infused by the power of the Sun god.*
>
> *That fasting in preparation of ceremony is righteous and for the consecration of this initiation taking place in a dark cave while reciting the "Hail Nymphus, hail New Light" mantra.*
>
> *The marital covenant entered wearing the "Veil of Reality", carrying the "Light of Truth" and pledge of celibacy is acceptable and Holy before God.*
>
> *That Venus is to be worshipped, along with the false god Mithras, with their defiled symbols of a chrysalis, mirror, bell, and diadem for this degree which surpass any other religious symbols.*

That transforming into a bee through a chrysalis is being reborn into a new and completely different life.

I ask that these false verdicts be overturned in the Courts of Heaven this day and replaced with righteous verdicts, and that I and my bloodlines be released from every bondage resulting from our involvement in the Title and Office of Bride of Mithras – Nymphus the Bridegroom, the Second Degree level of Mithraism.

Repentance

I repent for the participation and initiation in Nymphus, the Male Bride, the Second Degree of Mithraism with the offices, titles, regalia, oaths, vows, and initiation rites of this degree.

I repent for me and my bloodlines receiving the title and office of "Nymphus, the Male Bride."

I repent for all allegiance to Mithraism and surrender all membership into Mithras Orders over to Jesus Christ.

I repent for all worship of Venus or Mithras in any form or fashion and for all ungodly trades made with these false gods.

I repent for embracing the false verdict declaring:

The Office of Bride of Mithras (Nymphus the bridegroom) is a sacred office with all its oaths, vows, covenants, loyalty, eternality, and fidelity of this Second Degree and is in some fashion holy.

I repent for aligning myself with all the allegiances in this degree eternally.

I repent for joining myself and/or my ancestors joining our family to this false Bridegroom, making a mockery of the true Bridegroom and the Bride of Christ. Jesus is the Bridegroom, and we are the Bride of Christ. Isaiah 62:5 says,

> *For as a young man marries a virgin, so shall your sons marry you; and as the bridegroom rejoices over the bride, so shall your God rejoice over you.*

I repent for embracing the false verdict declaring:

> *The offering the cup representing my heart and water demonstrating my love to Mithras is holy.*

I repent for embracing this defilement of Holy Communion and the mockery of the sacrifice of Jesus Christ on the cross.

I repent for embracing the false verdict declaring:

> *The bread is infused by the power of the Sun god.*

I repent for receiving into my body or for those in my ancestral lines who partook of this defiled bread.

I repent for granting it power over my generations. Jesus Christ is the bread of life (John 6:35) and man shall not live by bread alone, but by every word that proceeds from the mouth of the God (Matthew 4:4).

I repent for embracing the false verdict declaring:

> *That fasting in preparation of ceremony is righteous and for the consecration of this initiation taking place*

> *in a dark cave while reciting the "Hail Nymphus, hail New Light" mantra.*

I repent for fasting to attain favor with the gods. I repent for attempting to find true light in darkness. Apart from You, Lord God, it is impossible to know truth because You (Jesus) are the way, the truth, and the life (John 14:6).

I repent for embracing the false verdict that declares:

> *The marital covenant entered wearing the "Veil of Reality", carrying the "Light of Truth" and pledge of celibacy and pledge of celibacy is acceptable and Holy before God.*

I repent for entering a false marriage by false means to obtain a false sense of belonging.

I repent for putting these false gods in Your place, Jesus. You are the Head, and I am part of the Body. I am part of the Bride and, Jesus, you have made it possible for me to be married to You, sharing an intimate, holy union by saving us from death and eternal separation from God. I have surrendered my heart and life to you Lord.

I repent for making a vow of celibacy and giving my seed only to Mithras. This vow contradicts your command to be "Be fruitful and multiply" (Genesis 1:22).

I recognize you as the True Light for Jesus is the Light of the World (John 8:12).

I repent for embracing the false verdict declaring:

> *That offering the cup representing my heart and water representing my love to Mithras and the bread is infused by the power of the Sun god.*

I repent for the unholy communion perpetrated by this ungodly covenant of offering my love and heart when You are the only sacrifice worth remembering in communion.

I repent for receiving the defiled bread in communion. You, Jesus, are the 'Bread of Life' and Life is only found in You.

I repent for embracing the false verdict declaring:

> *That Venus is to be worshipped along with the false god Mithras with their defiled symbols of a chrysalis, mirror, bell, and diadem for this degree which surpass any other religious symbols.*

I repent for giving worship and authority to these deities representing the planets that You created.

I repent for worship of created things whether animal, or otherwise. Your Word declares that "God is Spirit, and those who worship Him must worship in spirit and truth." (John 4:24). I know that Jesus gives me power and authority to trample over all power of the enemy and nothing by any means shall hurt me (Luke 10:19).

I repent for embracing the false verdict declaring:

> *Transforming into a bee through a chrysalis is being reborn into a new and completely different life.*

I repent for transforming into a different being other than the person you created me to be with a goal of a completely new life. This is an abominable practice to the Lord.

I repent for assuming this practice could bring me new life. I can only have a legitimate new life if I am reborn in Jesus Christ. (Acts 4:12)

Your Word says to not be conformed to this world, but be transformed by the renewing of your mind, that you may prove what is that good and acceptable and perfect will of God. (Romans 12:2).

* * * * *

You also may be impressed to go further with your repentance. Following Holy Spirit's leading here and as you go through the courtroom scenarios related to Mithraism.

Forgiveness

I forgive those human agents of darkness who devised and formulated this false religion without regard for, or despite, Your holy commandments. I forgive, bless, and release them in Jesus name. I forgive as I have been forgiven.

I forgive every ancestor who tied me to the covenants of Mithraism at any and every level, at any time, in any dimension. I release them this day from their guilt.

I ask forgiveness for any actions that introduced trauma into me and my bloodlines.

I ask that the trauma and fear be removed, in Jesus' name.

I forgive these ancestors for introducing this wickedness into my bloodline and I also forgive those who perpetuated it throughout the generations.

I forgive, bless, and release each of these persons, in Jesus' name.

Requests

I also request an absolute divorce from the false god Mithra and a severing of every tie to this false deity in whatever representation it held, at whatever time it occurred, and in whatever dimension it occurred.

I request that every fragment of my soul or my spirit, every captured part of my, or my ancestry's, DNA be regathered and restored unto me and my bloodlines, including everyone related to me by blood, marriage, adoption, civil, or religious covenants all the way back to the hand of the Father and all the way forward as far as it needs to go.

I request immediate release for me and my family, and the immediate release of everyone in my bloodlines that have been taken captive by these false verdicts. I also ask that the false identities perpetrated by this degree be voided in Jesus name.

I request complete release for my soul and spirit from all evil spirits, demons, evil entities, principalities, and powers thrust upon us at this degree.

I ask that these false verdicts be overturned in the Courts of Heaven this day and replaced with righteous verdicts, and that I, and my bloodlines, be released from every bondage resulting from my involvement in the Second Degree level of Mithraism.

I request that every ungodly trade be cancelled, and every form of taxation be lifted from me and my bloodlines.

I request that every aspect of this degree alleging eternality be cancelled, in Jesus' name.

I request the cancellation of every impact and ramification of the allegiances, covenants, oaths, vows, or dedications to Mithraism through this Second Degree in Jesus' name.

Additionally, I request that all these actions be applied to everyone related to me by blood, marriage, adoption, civil or religious covenant, all the way back to the hand of the Father and all the way forward as far as it needs to go, in Jesus' mighty name.

Conclusion

Today, I stand as a representative of my bloodline in Your Court. I request that the repentance for my bloodline be recorded in all pertinent courts, be used in other pertinent court cases, and be recorded in the books of Heaven for me and for my generations. I also request the immediate release of the Lord's blessings that have been held back or lost to me and my generations because of connections to Mithraism.

I thank you Just Judge and this court for hearing my repentance and requests this day and I request these things today in the Courts of Heaven, in Jesus' name.

Prayed this ____ day of _____, _____.

By _____

Further Instructions

Now, as you await the verdict, listen carefully for any further instructions you may be given. Once a favorable verdict is rendered, you will sense a flood of peace into your being. You may also experience other manifestations as the formerly attached entities make their exit from your life. Rejoice with gratitude for the new level of freedom you will now experience!

As a prophetic act, remove the symbolic marriage ring and give it to the angel attending you. Also, remove any regalia[6] associated with this degree, handing it to the angel for disposal.

You also may be impressed to go further with your repentance. Follow Holy Spirit's leading here and as you go through the remaining Courtroom Scenarios related to Mithraism.

---

[6] Regalia – special garments worn in ceremonial situations. May include special jewelry or headgear.

Chapter 5
Third Degree

Miles, the Soldier

In the Third Degree, known as the Miles the Soldier degree, under the protection of the planet Mars, the false gods worshipped are Mithras and Mars, and the ritual symbols were the soldier's kit bag, helmet, lance, drum, belt, and breastplate.

Courtroom Scenario

In Jesus' name, I request access to the Appeals Court of Heaven.

Just Judge, I stand here on behalf of myself [state your full name] and on behalf of my bloodlines – past, present, and future – everyone related to me by blood, marriage, adoption, civil or religious covenant.

I also ask that my cloud of witnesses be allowed to be present in the courtroom today.

False Verdicts

I ask that the false verdicts entered into at the "Miles the Soldier" degree, which is the Third Degree, be replaced with righteous verdicts on my behalf and on behalf of my bloodlines, in Jesus' name.

These false verdicts are as follows:

> *Participation and initiation in "Miles the Soldier" – the Third Degree of Mithraism with the offices, titles, regalia, oaths, vows, and initiation rites of this degree including kneeling naked before the altar of Mithras after being bound and blindfolded is an acceptable practice in the sight of the Lord.*
>
> *Submitting to and worshipping the planet Mars (god of war), Mithras, and "Miles the Soldier", giving them authority over me (and my lineage) is a holy thing.*
>
> *Reciting the false verdict of "Mithras is my only crown."*
>
> *I am the property of Mithra. That by being branded, tattooed, or marked, I signify this ownership claim.*
>
> *Believing true liberty is in Mithraism. Promoting its symbols of armor – helmet, kit bag, belt, lance, drum, and breastplate as vices of power from Mithras.*

Repentance

I repent for all allegiance to Mithraism and surrender all membership into Mithras Orders over to Jesus Christ.

I repent for all worship of Mars, Mithras, Miles the Soldier or any other false deity in any form or fashion, and for all ungodly trades made with these false gods.

I repent for participation and initiation in Miles the Soldier – the Third Degree of Mithraism – with the offices, titles, regalia, oaths, vows, and initiation rites of this degree.

I repent for me and my bloodlines receiving the title and office of "Miles the Soldier."

I repent for participating in and accepting the titles, offices, oaths, vows, and initiation rites of the Third Degree of Mithraism.

I repent for embracing the false verdict declaring:

> *That kneeling naked before the altar of Mithras after being bound and blindfolded is an acceptable practice in the sight of the Lord.*

I repent for kneeling naked in reverence to Mithras. I think of how Adam and Eve were naked and not ashamed in the garden and that is how I present myself before you in spirit. I bow before You because I cannot stand in Your Presence – You are too Holy.

I repent for being led astray by the power of protection presented by "Miles the Soldier" promised at this degree of Mithraism. I recognize that the Lord is my protector, He prepares a table before me in the presence of my enemies, whom shall I fear, He is my shield and fortress, in Him will I trust (Psalm 23:4-5, 91:2).

I repent for embracing the false verdict declaring:

> *Submitting to and worshipping the planet Mars (god of war), Mithras, and "Miles the Soldier" and giving them authority over me (and my bloodline) as well as reciting "Mithras is my only crown," and promoting its symbols of armor – helmet, kit bag, belt, lance, drum, and breastplate as vices of power from Mithras is acceptable before you, LORD God.*

I repent for paying homage to the deities in this degree and agreeing to give them my loyalty because I need their protection. The Lord is my refuge and my fortress, I can hide under the shadow of the Almighty; He is always with me to protect me. My lovingkindness and my fortress, my high tower and my deliverer, my shield and the one in whom I take refuge, and who subdues my people under me. (Psalm 91:1-2, 144:2)

I repent for embracing the false verdict declaring:

> *I am the property of Mithra. That by being branded, tattooed, or marked, I signify this ownership claim.*

I repent for being branded, tattooed, or marked for ownership to the deities involved in this degree.

I repent for not allowing Jehovah-Nissi to be my Banner. He fights all my battles for me. He is my King, and I am forever washed by the Blood of the Lamb.

I repent for embracing the false verdict of:

> *Believing true liberty is in Mithraism. Promoting its symbols of armor – helmet, kit bag, belt, lance, drum, and breastplate as vices of power from Mithras.*

I repent for believing liberty is in Mithraism, for only in Christ is there true liberty and freedom. "Now the Lord is the Spirit, and where the Spirit of the Lord is, there is liberty [emancipation from bondage, true freedom]". (2 Corinthians 3:17) (AMP)

* * * * *

You also may be impressed to go further with your repentance. Follow Holy Spirit's leading here and as you go through the courtroom scenarios related to Mithraism.

Forgiveness

I forgive those human agents of darkness who devised and formulated this false religion without regard for, or despite, Your holy commandments. I forgive, bless, and release them in Jesus name. I forgive as I have been forgiven.

I forgive every ancestor who tied me to the covenants of Mithraism at any and every level, at any time, in any dimension. I release them this day from their guilt.

I ask forgiveness for any actions that introduced trauma into me and my bloodlines.

I ask that the trauma and fear be removed, in Jesus' name.

I forgive these ancestors for introducing this wickedness into my bloodline and I also forgive those who perpetuated it throughout the generations.

I forgive, bless, and release each of these persons, in Jesus' name.

Requests

I ask that these false verdicts be overturned in the Courts of Heaven this day and replaced with righteous verdicts, and that I and my bloodlines be released from every bondage resulting from our involvement in the Third Degree level of Mithraism.

I request my and my family's immediate release, and the immediate release of everyone in my bloodlines, that have been taken captive by these false verdicts.

I request that every ungodly trade be cancelled, and every form of taxation be lifted from me and my bloodlines.

Additionally, I request that all these actions be applied to everyone related to me by blood, marriage, adoption, civil or religious covenant, all the way back to the hand of the Father and all the way forward as far as it needs to go, in Jesus' mighty name.

Conclusion

Today, I stand as a representative of my bloodline in Your Court. I request that the repentance for my bloodline be recorded in all pertinent courts, be used in other pertinent court cases, and be recorded in the books of Heaven for me and for my generations. I also request the immediate release of the Lord's blessings that have been held back or lost to me and my generations because of connections to Mithraism.

I thank you Just Judge and this court for hearing my repentance and requests this day and I request these things today in the Courts of Heaven, in Jesus' name.

Prayed this ____ day of _____, _____.

By _____

Further Instructions

Now, as you await the verdict, listen carefully for any further instructions you may be given. Once a favorable verdict is rendered, you will sense a flood of peace into your being. You may also experience other manifestations as the formerly attached entities make their exit from your life. Rejoice with gratitude for the new level of freedom you will now experience!

As a prophetic act, remove the symbolic marriage ring and give it to the angel attending you. Also, remove any regalia[7] associated with this degree handing it to the angel.

You also may be impressed to go further with your repentance. Follow Holy Spirit's leading here and as you go through the remaining courtroom scenarios related to Mithraism.

---

[7] Regalia – special garments worn in ceremonial situations. May include special jewelry or headgear.

Chapter 6
Fourth Degree

Leo, the Lion

Known as the Leo the Lion degree, in the Fourth Degree one is supposedly under the protection of the planet Jupiter. The false gods worshipped are the Leontocephaline and Jupiter. The ritual symbols were the small hand shovel, sistrum (a musical instrument), laurel wreath, and thunderbolts.

Courtroom Scenario

In Jesus' name, I request access to the Appeals Court of Heaven.

Just Judge, I stand here on behalf of myself _[state your full name]_ and on behalf of my bloodlines – past, present, and future – everyone related to me by blood, marriage, adoption, civil or religious covenant.

I also ask that my cloud of witnesses be allowed to be present in the courtroom today.

False Verdicts

I ask that the false verdicts entered into at the "Leo, the Lion" degree, which is the Fourth Degree, be replaced with righteous verdicts on my behalf and on behalf of my bloodlines, in Jesus' name.

These false verdicts are as follows:

> *By participation in the Fourth Degree, "Leo the Lion", using shape-shifting and shamanism enactments, I become "one" with the lion spirit and worshipping the lion spirit and/or worshipping lions carrying in "the last supper" is a holy thing.*
>
> *Mithras's last supper of bread and wine with his companions ('the Brotherhood') before his ascent into the heavens in Sol's (the Sun god) golden chariot is the mark of a true savior. "The Brotherhood" will let me know what to do.*
>
> *Red honey provides purification from guilt. The anointing honey is used for the initiates tongue, and to wash his hands to prepare for the fire ritual with the "ordeal pit".*
>
> *Taking care of the sacred flame and burning incense to these gods is holy.*
>
> *Worshipping and submitting to Leontocephaline, with the snake wrapped around his body, holding the keys to the kingdom, and astral travel wings makes me a god, and I must worship the planet Jupiter (god of strength).*

I repent for embracing the false verdict declaring that:

> *By participation in the Fourth Degree, "Leo the Lion", using shape-shifting and shamanism enactments, I become "one" with the lion spirit and worshipping the lion spirit and/or worshipping lions carrying in "the last supper" is a holy thing.*

I repent for seeking to be one with Leo the Lion or any lion spirit. You, Lord Jesus are the Lion of the Tribe of Judah and allegiance should only go to you.

I repent for using shape shifting and shamanism enactments to become one with the lion spirit.

I repent for worshipping the lion spirit.

I repent for worshipping lions.

I repent for embracing their involvement in the ritual of the last supper and for embracing that any of these acts or deeds was a holy thing. They were abominable to you Lord God.

I repent for embracing the false verdict declaring:

> *Mithras's last supper of bread and wine with his companions ('the Brotherhood') before his ascent into the heavens in Sol's (the Sun god) golden chariot is the mark of a true savior. "The Brotherhood" will let me know what to do.*

I repent for the "last supper" and false communion of the Fourth Degree with "the Brotherhood", which represents spiritual leadership to me and my lineage.

I repent for allowing "the Brotherhood" to control me and my lineage and placing them on a pedestal above You - Just Judge, Lord Jesus, and Holy Spirit.

I repent for all regalia associated with Sol the Sun god, as transferred over to my understanding of vestments of honor for men in leadership and or Mithras priests. I ask the blood of Jesus to be poured over all regalia in order to sever all soul ties acquired during this Fourth Degree.

Mark 12:29-31 says, "Jesus answered him, "The first of the commandments is: 'Hear, O Israel, the Lord our God, the Lord is one. 30 And you shall love the Lord your God with all your heart, with all your soul, with all your mind, and with all your strength.' This is the first commandment. 31 And the second, like it, is this: 'You shall love your neighbor as yourself.' There is no other commandment greater than these."

I repent for embracing the false verdict declaring:

> *Red honey is used for purification from guilt. The anointing honey is used for the initiates tongue and to wash his hands to prepare for the fire ritual with the "ordeal pit".*

I repent for the false purification anointing of honey in the fire initiation. I declare that only Christ's blood purifies sin.

I repent for the worship of fire and looking to fire for power and protection, when faith should not be in the wisdom of men but in the power of God. (1 Corinthians 2:5)

I repent for embracing the false verdict declaring:

> *Taking care of the sacred flame and burning incense to these gods is holy.*

I repent for tending the sacred flame and burning incense to the gods of this degree. My God is a consuming fire. He reigns down fire from heaven. He is so powerful. His voice divides the flames of the fire. He will baptize you with the Holy Spirit and fire. (Matthew 3:11) (NASB)

I repent for embracing the false verdict declaring:

> *Worshipping and submitting to Leontocephaline, with the snake wrapped around his body, holding the keys to the kingdom, and astral travel wings makes me a god, and I must worship the planet Jupiter (god of strength).*

I repent for submitting to and worshipping Jupiter, god of strength. I know the joy of the Lord is my strength.

I repent for submitting my will to Leontocephaline, a snake, false kingdom keys and astral wings. Leontocephaline is a principality, and the snake is crushed under Jesus' heel. I, being a child of God, have the Keys to the Kingdom, I hide under the shadow of the Almighty God, and under His wings I shall take refuge.

Repentance

I repent for the participation and initiation in this Fourth Degree, "Leo the Lion" using shape-shifting and shamanism enactments to become "one" with the lion spirit and for worshipping the Lion spirit (including lions) carrying in "the last supper."

I repent for shapeshifting into the lion.

I repent for worshipping the lion and bringing evil into me and my bloodlines. Jesus, I ask that you separate me, and my generations spirits and souls, from the entities allowed into us because of the shape-shifting and shamanism in this degree.

I repent for worshipping a lion spirit, for Jesus is the Lion of Judah, He is the only One worthy of worship.

I repent for bringing in the feast as a ritual lion. This is wicked and false, a cheap imitation of the true Lion–Jesus. Jesus is the Lion King (Revelation 5:5).

I repent for the use of the sistrum to create frequencies not pleasing to the LORD of Hosts.

I repent for giving me and my lineage over to altars of Leo the lion, lion spirit, Jupiter and any other evil entity or identity of protection related to this degree.

I repent for participation and initiation into the Leo, the Lion, the Fourth Degree of Mithraism.

I repent for embracing the offices, titles, regalia, oaths, vows, and initiation rites of this degree.

I repent for me and my bloodlines receiving the title and office of "Leo, the Lion."

I repent for participating in and accepting the titles, offices, oaths, vows, and initiation rites of the Fourth Degree of Mithraism.

I repent for all allegiance to Mithraism and surrender all membership into Mithras Orders over to Jesus Christ.

I repent for all worship of the Leontocephaline in any form or fashion and for all ungodly trades made with these false gods.

* * * * *

You also may be impressed to go further with your repentance. Follow Holy Spirit's leading here and as you go through the courtroom scenarios related to Mithraism.

Forgiveness

I forgive those human agents of darkness who devised and formulated this false religion without regard for, or despite, Your holy commandments. I forgive, bless, and release them in Jesus name. I forgive as I have been forgiven.

I forgive every ancestor who tied me to the covenants of Mithraism at any and every level, at any time, in any dimension. I release them this day from their guilt.

I ask forgiveness for any actions that introduced trauma into me and my bloodlines.

I ask that the trauma and fear be removed, in Jesus' name.

I forgive these ancestors for introducing this wickedness into my bloodline and I also forgive those who perpetuated it throughout the generations.

I forgive, bless, and release each of these persons, in Jesus' name.

Requests

I ask that these false verdicts be overturned in the Courts of Heaven this day and replaced with righteous verdicts, and that I, and my bloodlines, be released from every bondage resulting from my involvement in the Fourth Degree level of Mithraism.

I also request an absolute divorce from the false god Mithra and a severing of every tie to this false god in whatever representation it held, at whatever time it occurred, and in whatever dimension it occurred.

I request that every ungodly trade be cancelled, and every form of taxation be lifted from me and my bloodlines.

I request the cancellation of every impact and ramification of the allegiances, covenants, oaths, vows, or dedications to Mithraism through this Fourth Degree, in Jesus' name.

I request my, and my family's, immediate release, and the immediate release of everyone in my bloodlines that have been taken captive by these false verdicts. I ask for complete restoration from the trauma of the "ordeal pit" and all traumas related to the rituals participated in this degree.

Additionally, I request that all these actions be applied to everyone related to me by blood, marriage, adoption, civil or religious covenant, all the way back to the hand of the Father and all the way forward as far as it needs to go, in Jesus' mighty name.

Conclusion

Today, I stand as a representative of my bloodline in Your Court. I request that the repentance for my bloodline be recorded in all pertinent courts, be used in other pertinent court cases, and be recorded in the books of Heaven for me and for my generations. I also request the immediate release of the Lord's blessings that have been held back or lost to me and my generations because of connections to Mithraism.

I thank you Just Judge and this court for hearing my repentance and requests this day and I request these things today in the Courts of Heaven, in Jesus' name.

Prayed this ____ day of _____, _____.

By _____

Further Instructions

Now, as you await the verdict, listen carefully for any further instructions you may be given. Once a favorable verdict is rendered, you will sense a flood of peace into your being. You may also experience other manifestations as the formerly attached entities make their exit from your life. Rejoice with gratitude for the new level of freedom you will now experience!

As a prophetic act, remove the symbolic marriage ring and give it to the angel attending you. Also, remove any regalia[8] associated with this degree handing it to the angel.

You also may be impressed to go further with your repentance. Follow Holy Spirit's leading here and as you go through the courtroom scenarios related to Mithraism.

---

[8] Regalia – special garments worn in ceremonial situations. May include special jewelry or headgear.

Chapter 7
Fifth Degree

Peres/Perseus, the Persian

In the Fifth Degree known as the Peres or Perseus - the Persian, one is under the protection of the moon. The false god worshipped is the Prince of Persia & Perseus, and the ritual symbols are the Phrygian[9] cap, sickle, moon, stars, and the sling pouch.

Courtroom Scenario

In Jesus' name, I request access to the Appeals Court of Heaven.

Just Judge, I stand here on behalf of myself [state your full name] and on behalf of my bloodlines – past, present, and future – everyone related to me by blood, marriage, adoption, civil or religious covenant.

---

[9] A Phrygian cap is pointed in the front. It was often depicted as the type of cap worn by Robin Hood.

I also ask that my cloud of witnesses be allowed to be present in the courtroom today.

False Verdicts

I ask that the false verdicts entered into at the "Peres/Perseus – the Persian" the Fifth Degree be replaced with righteous verdicts on my behalf and on behalf of my bloodlines, in Jesus' name.

These false verdicts are as follows:

> *Participation and initiation into this Fifth Degree of "Peres/Perseus the Persian" as a sign of prowess and power is a holy thing.*
>
> *The worship of the Moon god (Allah) and Prince of Persia (Perseus), and using fertility rites by the moon, is acceptable and necessary worship.*
>
> *Entering marital covenant with "the Persian" to obtain royal Persian bloodline rites is a holy thing.*
>
> *Using honey for purification in this degree's ritual, causing the word "honeymoon" to come from this level of Mithraism, is holy.*
>
> *The symbols of this degree including wearing the Phrygian cap, sling pouch and any other regalia to depict this degree offer prestige and power and are holy.*

I ask that these false verdicts be overturned in the Courts of Heaven this day and replaced with righteous verdicts, and that I, and my bloodlines, be released from every bondage resulting from my involvement in the Fifth Degree level of Mithraism.

Repentance

I repent for participation and initiation in Peres/Perseus, the Persian, the Fifth Degree of Mithraism with the offices, titles, regalia, oaths, vows, and initiation rites of this degree.

I repent for me and my bloodlines receiving the title and office of "Peres/Perseus, the Persian."

I repent for accepting the titles, offices, oaths, vows, and initiation rites of the Fifth Degree of Mithraism.

I repent for all allegiance to Mithraism and surrender all membership into Mithras Orders over to Jesus Christ.

I repent for all worship of the moon, or the Prince of Persia or Perseus, in any form or fashion, and for all ungodly trades made with these false gods.

I repent on behalf of me and my bloodlines spirit, soul, and body, receiving the title and office of "Peres/Perseus – the Persian."

I repent for embracing the false verdict declaring:

> *Participation and initiation into this Fifth Degree of "Peres/Perseus the Persian" as a sign of prowess and power is a holy thing.*

I repent for looking to the star constellation, Perseus the Persian, a sickle or any other gods for power and prowess.

"Bless the LORD, O my soul! O LORD my God, You are very great: You are clothed with honor and majesty, ²Who covers Yourself with light as with a garment, who stretch out the heavens like a curtain (Psalm 104:1-2). Your Spirit, O Lord is greater than any contrived power of earth or the heavens. You do things not by power or by might but by Your Spirit (Zechariah 4:6).

I repent for embracing the false verdict declaring:

> *The worship of the Moon god (Allah) and Prince of Persia (Perseus), and using fertility rites by the moon, is acceptable and necessary worship.*

I repent for the profane worship of the moon god, Allah, the "Prince of Persia" and all principalities at this degree.

I repent for participating in fertility rites in this degree. My fidelity and devotion belong to You Lord. You Lord are the Alpha and Omega, the beginning, and the end, for Yours is the Power, the Honor, the Glory, and the Kingdom forever!

I repent for embracing the false verdict declaring:

> *Entering marital covenant with "the Persian" to obtain royal Persian bloodline rites is a holy thing.*

I repent for participating in an unholy union such as this.

I repent for agreeing to it or cooperating with it on any level.

I repent for the participation, dedications, and consummation of this unholy marriage to "the Persian" in this degree.

I repent for the occultic soul ties that resulted from this level of Mithraism.

I am part of the Bride of Christ, He is my Betrothed, I have been grafted into a royal priesthood, a holy nation, His own special person, that I may proclaim the praises of Him who called me out of darkness into His marvelous light. (I Peter 2:9)

I repent for embracing the false verdict declaring:

> *Using honey for purification in this degree's ritual causing the word "honeymoon" to come from this level of Mithraism is holy.*

I repent for the perverted use of honey in the purification ceremony.

I repent for embracing the false verdict declaring:

> *The symbols of this degree including wearing the Phrygian cap, sling pouch and any other regalia to depict this degree offer prestige and power and are holy.*

I repent for the symbols: Phrygian cap, sling pouch and any other regalia, for I have been clothed in the righteousness of God in Christ and put on the whole armor of God to resist the wiles of the devil.

* * * * *

You also may be impressed to go further with your repentance. Follow Holy Spirit's leading here and as you go through the remaining courtroom scenarios related to Mithraism.

Forgiveness

I forgive those human agents of darkness who devised and formulated this false religion without regard for, or despite, Your holy commandments. I forgive, bless, and release them in Jesus name. I forgive as I have been forgiven.

I forgive every ancestor who tied me to the covenants of Mithraism at any and every level, at any time, in any dimension. I release them this day from their guilt.

I ask forgiveness for any actions that introduced trauma into me and my bloodlines.

I ask that the trauma and fear be removed, in Jesus' name.

I forgive these ancestors for introducing this wickedness into my bloodline and I also forgive those who perpetuated it throughout the generations.

I forgive, bless, and release each of these persons, in Jesus' name.

Requests

I ask that these false verdicts be overturned in the Courts of Heaven this day and replaced with righteous verdicts, and that I, and my bloodlines, be released from every bondage resulting from my involvement in the Fifth Degree level of Mithraism.

I request an absolute divorce from the false god Mithra and a severing of every tie to this false god in whatever representation it held, at whatever time it occurred, and in whatever dimension it occurred.

I request that every fragment of my soul or my spirit, every captured part of my, or my ancestry's, DNA be regathered and restored unto me and my bloodlines, including everyone related to me by blood, marriage, adoption, civil, or religious covenants all the way back to the hand of the Father and all the way forward as far as it needs to go.

I request that every ungodly trade be cancelled, and every form of taxation be lifted from me and my bloodlines.

I request the cancellation of every impact and ramification of the allegiances, covenants, oaths, vows, or dedications to Mithraism through this Fifth Degree, in Jesus' name.

I request my and my family's immediate release and the immediate release of everyone in my bloodlines that have been taken captive by these false verdicts.

I ask for complete restoration from all traumas related to the rituals participated in for this degree.

Additionally, I request that all these actions be applied to everyone related to me by blood, marriage, adoption, civil or religious covenant, all the way back to the hand of the Father and all the way forward as far as it needs to go, in Jesus' mighty name.

Conclusion

Today, I stand as a representative of my bloodline in Your Court. I request that the repentance for my bloodline be recorded in all pertinent courts, be used in other pertinent court cases, and be recorded in the books of Heaven for me and for my generations. I also request the immediate release of the Lord's blessings that have been held back or lost to me and my generations because of connections to Mithraism.

I thank you Just Judge and this court for hearing my repentance and requests this day and I request these things today in the Courts of Heaven, in Jesus' name.

Prayed this ____ day of _____, _____.

By _____

Further Instructions

Now, as you await the verdict, listen carefully for any further instructions you may be given. Once a favorable verdict is rendered, you will sense a flood of peace into your being. You may also experience other manifestations as the formerly attached entities make their exit from your life. Rejoice with gratitude for the new level of freedom you will now experience!

As a prophetic act, remove the symbolic marriage ring and give it to the angel attending you. Also, remove any regalia[10] associated with this degree handing it to the angel.

You may be impressed to go further with your repentance. Follow Holy Spirit's leading here and as you go through the remaining courtroom scenarios related to Mithraism.

---

[10] Regalia – special garments worn in ceremonial situations. May include special jewelry or headgear.

Chapter 8
Sixth Degree

Heliodromus, the Sun Runner

In the Sixth Degree known as the Heliodromus, the Sun Runner degree, the participant is placed under the protection of the sun. The false gods worshipped are Sol Invictus and Helios, while the ritual symbols are the torch, the chariot, whip, and robes.

Courtroom Scenario

In Jesus' name, I request access to the Appeals Court of Heaven.

Just Judge, I stand here on behalf of myself _[state your full name]_ and on behalf of my bloodlines – past, present, and future – everyone related to me by blood, marriage, adoption, civil or religious covenant.

I also ask that my cloud of witnesses be allowed to be present in the courtroom today.

False Verdicts

I ask that the false verdicts entered into at the "Heliodromus the Sun Runner" degree, which is the Sixth Degree, be replaced with righteous verdicts on my behalf and on behalf of my bloodlines, in Jesus' name.

These false verdicts are as follows:

> *The participation and initiation into this Sixth Degree of "Heliodromus the Sun Runner" is a holy thing.*
>
> *Worship of the sun and Heliodromus is a holy thing.*
>
> *Submitting to the authority of the principalities and powers of this degree, such as Sol Invictus, with sunbeams coming from his head, is a holy thing.*
>
> *I can use the symbols (torch of light, chariot, whip, and red robes of Helios) to gain power over others and gain spiritual power with the Mithras sect. This is acceptable before the Lord God of Hosts.*
>
> *The red color to represent sun, fire, and blood, is representative of royalty.*
>
> *Communion of bull's blood can atone for my sins, next to the sacrificed bull carcass.*

Repentance

I repent for the participation and initiation in the Heliodromus, the Sun Runner degree, the Sixth Degree of Mithraism with the offices, titles, regalia, oaths, vows, and initiation rites of this degree.

I repent for worshipping the Sun, Sol Invictus, and invoking the anti-Christ entities represented in this degree.

I repent for submitting to the principalities and powers of this degree. Christ is the true head and there is no other greater, Ephesians 5:23 says, "Christ is head of the church; and He is the Savior of the body...." "...and the head of Christ is God." (1 Corinthians 11:3)

I repent on behalf of me and my bloodlines receiving the title and office of "Heliodromus the Sun Runner."

I repent for participating in and accepting the titles, offices, oaths, vows, and initiation rites of the Sixth Degree of Mithraism.

I repent for embracing the false verdict that the worship of the sun and Heliodromus is a holy thing. Your Word declares that I am to have no other gods beside You.

I repent for all worship of the sun, Sol Invictus, or Helios in any form or fashion, and for all ungodly trades made with these false gods.

I repent for submitting to Sol Invictus, Helios, or the sun in any fashion.

I repent for embracing the false verdict declaring:

> *I can use the symbols (torch of light, chariot, whip, and red robes of Helios) to gain power over others and gain spiritual power with the Mithras sect, and that it is acceptable before the Lord God of Hosts.*

I repent for using the Torch of Light as an extension of the sun. There is only One Light of the world and that's Jesus.

I repent for using the chariot and whip to symbolize wealth and power to others on earth. My Father owns the cattle on a thousand hills, so why do I need to impress people when He owns it all anyway. He is the One who gives and takes away.

I repent for embracing the false verdict declaring:

> *The red color to represent sun, fire, and blood, is representative of royalty.*

I repent for the wearing of the red robes that are symbolic of the blood of the bull. Only the blood of Christ washes away sin and because of Him I and my bloodlines are part of a royal priesthood.

I repent for agreeing with the false verdicts that red in the Mithraic ceremonies is a royal color.

I repent for embracing the false verdict declaring:

> *Communion of bull's blood can atone for my sins, next to the sacrificed bull carcass.*

I repent for the ritual sacrifice of the bull and for drinking bull's blood in an unholy communion.

I repent for feasting on meat sacrificed to the deities of this level of Mithraism. True righteous communion only takes place with Father, Son, Holy Spirit and me and my bloodlines who have devoted themselves to You, Jesus.

I repent for all allegiance to Mithraism and surrender all membership into Mithras Orders over to Jesus Christ.

* * * * *

You also may be impressed to go further with your repentance. Follow Holy Spirit's leading here and as you go through the remaining courtroom scenarios related to Mithraism.

Forgiveness

I forgive those human agents of darkness who devised and formulated this false religion without regard for, or despite, Your holy commandments. I forgive, bless, and release them in Jesus name. I forgive as I have been forgiven.

I forgive every ancestor who tied me to the covenants of Mithraism at any and every level, at any time, in any dimension. I release them this day from their guilt.

I ask forgiveness for any actions that introduced trauma into me and my bloodlines.

I ask that the trauma and fear be removed, in Jesus' name.

I forgive these ancestors for introducing this wickedness into my bloodline and I also forgive those who perpetuated it throughout the generations.

I forgive, bless, and release each of these persons, in Jesus' name.

Requests

I ask that these false verdicts be overturned in the Courts of Heaven this day and replaced with righteous verdicts, and that I, and my bloodlines, be released from every bondage resulting from our involvement in the Sixth Degree level of Mithraism.

I request angelic assistance in casting out every evil spirit, unclean spirit, demon, principality, and evil entity that entered my bloodline by blood, marriage covenant (civil or religious or adoption) spirit, soul, and body during this Sixth Degree of "Heliodromus the Sun Runner". For every Lingering Human Spirit[11], I ask that the silver channel be opened, and each spirit be taken to judgment in mercy.

I request my, and my family's, immediate release, and the immediate release of everyone in my bloodlines that have been taken captive by these false verdicts.

Additionally, I request that all these actions be applied to everyone related to me by blood, marriage, adoption, civil or religious covenant, all the way back to the hand of the Father and all the way forward as far as it needs to go, in Jesus' mighty name.

Conclusion

Today, I stand as a representative of my bloodline in Your Court. I request that the repentance for my bloodline be recorded in all pertinent courts, be used in other pertinent court cases, and be recorded in the books of Heaven for me and for my generations. I also request the immediate release of the Lord's blessings that have been held back or lost to me and my generations because of connections to Mithraism.

---

[11] See *A Simple Explanation of Lingering Human Spirits* in the Appendix.

I thank you Just Judge and this court for hearing my repentance and requests this day and I request these things today in the Courts of Heaven, in Jesus' name.

Prayed this ____ day of _____, _____.

By _____

Further Instructions

Now, as you await the verdict, listen carefully for any further instructions you may be given. Once a favorable verdict is rendered, you will sense a flood of peace into your being. You may also experience other manifestations as the formerly attached entities make their exit from your life. Rejoice with gratitude for the new level of freedom you will now experience!

As a prophetic act, remove the symbolic marriage ring and give it to the angel attending you. Also, remove any regalia[12] associated with this degree handing it to the angel.

You also may be impressed to go further with your repentance. Follow Holy Spirit's leading here and as you go through the remaining courtroom scenarios related to Mithraism.

---

[12] Regalia – special garments worn in ceremonial situations. May include special jewelry or headgear.

Chapter 9
Seventh Degree

Pater, the Father

Known as the Pater, the Father degree, in this Seventh Degree (also the final degree), the participant is placed under the protection of the planet Saturn. The false god worshipped is Satan, and the ritual symbols were the mitre, shepherd's staff, ruby ring, cape/mantle, and elaborate jewel encrusted robes with metallic threads.

Courtroom Scenario

In Jesus' name, I request access to the Appeals Court of Heaven.

Just Judge, I stand here on behalf of myself [state your full name] and on behalf of my bloodlines – past, present, and future – everyone related to me by blood, marriage, adoption, civil or religious covenant.

I also ask that my cloud of witnesses be allowed to be present in the courtroom today.

False Verdicts

I ask that the false verdicts entered into at the "Pater the Father" degree, which is the Seventh Degree, be replaced with righteous verdicts on my behalf and on behalf of my bloodlines, in Jesus' name.

These false verdicts are as follows:

> *Participation, and initiation into this Seventh Degree of "Pater the Father" makes me a representative of Mithras as a man on earth and is a holy thing.*
>
> *Representing Pater, Saturn (god of dissolution, wealth, agriculture, and liberty) and Satan is sacred.*
>
> *Pater Patrum is the Father of Fathers.*
>
> *Pater Sacrorum is the Father of the Mysteries.*
>
> *Pater Nominus is the Father of the Conformity with Custom.*
>
> *Worshipping Pater and Saturn (Satan) and submitting to their authority at this degree, including marriage and blood covenants, is holy.*
>
> *All ordinations, coronations, sexual sin, and initiation rites in exchange for wealth, prestige and spiritual power is an exemplary practice.*
>
> *Human and animal sacrifices made in honor of the deities of this level are sacred.*
>
> *All the paraphernalia, regalia, and symbols of this degree - the Mitre, shepherd's staff, the ruby ring, mantle/cap, jewel encrusted robes and threads are regal and royal.*

I ask that these false verdicts be overturned in the Courts of Heaven this day and replaced with righteous verdicts, and that I, and my bloodlines, spirit, soul, and body, be released from every bondage resulting from our involvement in the Seventh Degree level of Mithraism.

Repentance

I repent for the participation and initiation in Pater, the Father, the Seventh Degree of Mithraism with the offices, titles, regalia, oaths, vows, and initiation rites of this degree.

I repent for me and my bloodlines receiving the title and office of "Pater, the Father."

I repent for participating in and accepting the titles, offices, oaths, vows, and initiation rites of the Seventh Degree of Mithraism.

I repent for all allegiance to Mithraism and surrender all membership into Mithras Orders over to Jesus Christ.

I repent for all worship of Saturn or Satan in any form or fashion, and for all ungodly trades made with these false gods.

I repent for embracing the false verdict declaring:

> *Participation, and initiation into this Seventh Degree of "Pater the Father" makes me a representative of Mithras as a man on earth and is a holy thing.*

I repent on behalf of me and my bloodlines receiving the title and office of "Pater the Father."

I repent for participating in and accepting the titles, offices, oaths, vows, and initiation rites of the Seventh Degree of Mithraism, indicating I have arrived at completion.

I repent for embracing the false verdicts declaring:

> *Representing Pater, Saturn (god of dissolution, wealth, agriculture, and liberty) and Satan is sacred.*
>
> *Pater Patrum is the Father of Fathers*
>
> *Pater Sacrorum is the Father of the Mysteries*
>
> *Pater Nominus is the Father of the Conformity with Custom*

I repent for representing "Pater Patrum the Father of Fathers", "Pater Sacrorum the Father of the Mysteries" and "Pater Nominus the Father of the Conformity with Custom". Each of these are a false Abba Father, a false father of secrets, and a false father of tradition - none of which come close to the GREAT I AM, who is also known as the Ancient of Days.

I repent for participating in an elaborate ruse to fool men into believing they can become as god. There is One true Father and, although You are called by many names in Your Word, the one that always speaks to me is the GREAT I AM. You are everything and in everything it is that You created. You are always creating; you are never stuck in tradition. You reveal mysteries if we walk closely to You. Those lesser gods do not compare to You, they have done nothing but attempt to shine in Your Light. Your Light is too bright to counterfeit. I worship You Father – the Ultimate Father.

I repent for embracing the false verdict declaring:

Worshipping Pater and Saturn (Satan) and submitting to their authority at this degree is acceptable before God.

I repent for all worship of the planet Saturn, the deity of Satan and Pater, and for submission to their authority.

I repent for every form of worship, blood covenant, ordination, and coronation to these pagan gods as well as the evil trades that my lineage and I made.

I repent for marriage covenants and sexual encounters with Pater, Saturn, and Satan.

I repent for saturating myself and my bloodlines in iniquity and sin. Jesus wash us clean with Your Blood. I put my hope and Trust in You Father God, You Jesus, and You Holy Spirit.

I repent for embracing the false verdict declaring:

Human and animal sacrifices made in honor of the deities of this level are sacred.

I repent for all sacrifices at this level. In God's Word, Psalm 106:37-38 says, "They even sacrificed their sons and their daughters to demons, 38 and shed innocent blood, the blood of their sons and daughters. These pagan practices are unacceptable to your LORD God. "

Psalm 106:44-48 declares, "Nevertheless He regarded their affliction, When He heard their cry; 45 And for their sake He remembered His covenant and relented according to the multitude of His mercies. 46 He also made them to be pitied by all those who carried them away captive. 47 Save us, O LORD our God, and gather us from among the Gentiles, to give thanks to Your holy name, to triumph in Your praise. [48] Blessed be the LORD God of Israel from everlasting to everlasting! And let all the people say, "Amen!" Praise the LORD!"

I repent for embracing the false verdict declaring:

All the paraphernalia, regalia, and symbols of this degree - the Mitre, shepherd's staff, the ruby ring, mantle/cap, jewel encrusted robes and threads are regal and royal.

I repent for honoring the paraphernalia, regalia, and symbols of this degree. You, Lord Jesus, are the good shepherd and You do not lead with Pomp and Circumstance.

I repent for the worship of mere men who were lifted before us, on behalf of me and my bloodlines. "For there is one God and one Mediator between God and men, the Man Christ Jesus" (1 Timothy 2:5)

I repent for worshipping and celebrating Your creations, such as hierarchy in the churches, people, animals, insects, celestial bodies, myself, fallen angels, hybrid beings and false gods.

I repent for every unholy altar built in my heart because of worshipping your creations.

* * * * *

You also may be impressed to go further with your repentance. Follow Holy Spirit's leading here and as you go through the courtroom scenarios related to Mithraism.

Forgiveness

I forgive those human agents of darkness who devised and formulated this false religion without regard for, or despite, Your holy commandments. I forgive, bless, and release them in Jesus name. I forgive as I have been forgiven.

I forgive every ancestor who tied me to the covenants of Mithraism at any and every level, at any time, in any dimension. I release them this day from their guilt.

I ask forgiveness for any actions that introduced trauma into me and my bloodlines.

I ask that the trauma and fear be removed, in Jesus' name.

I forgive these ancestors for introducing this wickedness into my bloodline and I also forgive those who perpetuated it throughout the generations.

I forgive, bless, and release each of these persons, in Jesus' name.

Requests

I ask that these false verdicts be overturned in the Courts of Heaven this day and replaced with righteous verdicts, and that I, and my bloodlines, be released from every bondage resulting from my involvement in the Seventh Degree level of Mithraism.

I request my, and my family's, immediate release, and the immediate release of everyone in my bloodlines that have been taken captive by these false verdicts. I ask that my, and my family's, DNA be restored to a place of wholeness, life, and freedom that was intended at creation. Reverse all the ramifications and impacts that all the 7 Degrees of Mithraism have had on my generations - past, present and future - spirit, soul, and body.

I ask that all soul ties and any other ungodly ties be severed and destroyed in the name of Jesus.

Additionally, I request that all these actions be applied to everyone related to me by blood, marriage, adoption, civil or religious covenant, all the way back to the hand of the Father and all the way forward as far as it needs to go, in Jesus' mighty name.

Conclusion

Today, I stand as a representative of my bloodline in Your Court. I request that the repentance for my bloodline be recorded in all pertinent courts, be used in other pertinent court cases, and be recorded in the books of Heaven for me and for my generations. I also request the immediate release of the Lord's blessings that have been held back or lost to me and my generations because of connections to Mithraism.

I thank you Just Judge and this court for hearing my repentance and requests this day and I request these things today in the Courts of Heaven, in Jesus' name.

Prayed this _____ day of _____, _____.

By _____

Further Instructions

Now, as you await the verdict, listen carefully for any further instructions you may be given. Once a favorable verdict is rendered, you will sense a flood of peace into your being. You may also experience other manifestations as the formerly attached entities make their exit from your life. Rejoice with gratitude for the new level of freedom you will now experience!

As a prophetic act, remove the symbolic marriage ring and give it to the angel attending you. Also, remove any regalia[13] associated with this degree, handing it to the angel for disposal.

You also may be impressed to go further with your repentance. Follow Holy Spirit's leading here and as you go through the remaining courtroom scenarios related to Mithraism.

---

[13] Regalia – special garments worn in ceremonial situations. May include special jewelry or headgear.

Chapter 10
Closing Prayer

Just Judge, Jesus, and Holy Spirit, we (my lineage and I) give You praise, honor, and glory this day. You have set us free from Mithraism by the Power and Might of Your Name. Thank You for the freedom, healing, and deliverance that you have given over the last few days. Thank you for being a revealer of truth and a redeemer to the masses. Thank You, Abba, for the victory You have brought this day.

Psalm 91

He who dwells in the secret place of the Most High
Shall abide under the shadow of the Almighty.
² I will say of the LORD, "He is my refuge and my fortress;
My God, in Him I will trust."

³ Surely He shall deliver you from the snare of the fowler
And from the perilous pestilence.
⁴ He shall cover you with His feathers,
And under His wings you shall take refuge;

His truth shall be your *shield and buckler.*
⁵ *You shall not be afraid of the terror by night,*
Nor *of the arrow* that *flies by day,*
⁶ Nor *of the pestilence* that *walks in darkness,*
Nor *of the destruction* that *lays waste at noonday.*

⁷ *A thousand may fall at your side,*
And ten thousand at your right hand;
But *it shall not come near you.*
⁸ *Only with your eyes shall you look,*
And see the reward of the wicked.

⁹ *Because you have made the* LORD, who is *my refuge,*
Even *the Most High, your dwelling place,*
¹⁰ *No evil shall befall you,*
Nor shall any plague come near your dwelling;
¹¹ *For He shall give His angels charge over you,*
To keep you in all your ways.
¹² *In* their *hands they shall bear you up,*
Lest you dash your foot against a stone.
¹³ *You shall tread upon the lion and the cobra,*
The young lion and the serpent you shall trample underfoot.

¹⁴ "Because he has set his love upon Me, therefore I will deliver him;
I will set him on high, because he has known My name.
¹⁵ *He shall call upon Me, and I will answer him;*
I will be *with him in trouble;*
I will deliver him and honor him.
¹⁶ *With long life I will satisfy him,*
And show him My salvation."

Psalm 23

David's poetic praise to God
1 The Lord is my best friend and my shepherd.
I always have more than enough.
2 He offers a resting place for me in his luxurious love.
His tracks take me to an oasis of peace, the quiet brook of bliss.
3 That's where he restores and revives my life.
He opens before me pathways to God's pleasure
and leads me along in his footsteps of righteousness
so that I can bring honor to his name.
4 Lord, even when your path takes me through
the valley of deepest darkness,
fear will never conquer me, for you already have!
You remain close to me and lead me through it all the way.
Your authority is my strength and my peace.
The comfort of your love takes away my fear.
I'll never be lonely, for you are near.
5 You become my delicious feast
even when my enemies dare to fight.
You anoint me with the fragrance of your Holy Spirit;
you give me all I can drink of you until my heart overflows.
6 So why would I fear the future?
For your goodness and love pursue me all the days of my life.
Then afterward, when my life is through,
I'll return to your glorious presence to be forever with you! (TPT)

Chapter 11
Final Instructions

Holy Spirit may direct you to repeat all or part of this book in order to effect the full cleansing of your bloodline from the vestiges of Mithraism. If so, simply repeat each courtroom scenario as He directs.

This is a wonderful opportunity to free your yourself and your bloodlines from this wicked, pagan religion. Invest the time and effort needed! See your ancestors as they are getting set free. Imagine the rejoicing in Heaven as your bloodlines are obtaining their freedom.

Catholicism was the major Christian religion at the time when Mithraism flourished, and thus inherited many practices from Mithraism. Some of these traditions were then borrowed from the Catholic church during the Protestant Reformation. In this manner, Mithraism has affected most, if not all, of the Christian religious denominations to some degree or another.

There are additional repentances that you may wish to perform related to the role of organized religion in your life or in the lives of your ancestors.

Repent for any embrace of false gods, or the worship of false gods within the church or within any form of religion – organized or not, knowingly, or unknowingly. Ultimately, worshipping any entity other than the Lord God Jehovah is worship of Lucifer.

Repent for each and every instance in which man was elevated to the role of godhead and revered as such.

Repent for kissing the hand or cheeks of the priests, bishops, pastors, or others in authority – as this was used as an ungodly trade (exchanging DNA) to create a wicked trading floor on which you are/were the currency. The purpose was to reinforce an allegiance to the priest as the ultimate voice of God in one's life – this goes beyond Scripture and creates ungodly bondages.

Repent for any unholy allegiance to false denominational gods that was created through infant baptism. You, or your ancestors, were not a conscious participant when your allegiance was assigned. Your parents did not ask your permission.

Repent for any unholy bondages created through catechism. Ask Holy Spirit to remove from your mind and DNA every false dogma and opinion of man that you embraced through the process of catechism and confirmation.

We have embraced many holidays without knowing their origins. We have embraced myths and teachings that are ungodly.

We are living in a time when things that have been hidden from the Body of Christ are beginning to be revealed. Rejoice that new levels of freedom are available to you today and resolve to do whatever is necessary for you to walk in the freedom that is being offered.

These bondages don't stop with the Catholic faith, but found themselves in some level in virtually every denominational (and even non-denominational) stream. The corruption and infection was quite thorough. Thankfully, what has been hidden from the Body of Christ is being revealed and as it is being revealed we are able to step into new levels of liberty.

Ask Holy Spirit to inform you of any other ungodly practices or traditions that have created bondage in your life or lineage. Repent when you are made aware of the issue and ask that the matter be restored according the will and purposes of God for your life and family. Ask Holy Spirit to be your ultimate teacher and guide you into all truth. He will gladly do so.

Chapter 12
The Court of Reclamations

Now that you have worked through the process of gaining freedom from the clutches of Mithraism, you need to get back what you have lost to the enemy. Heaven recently introduced us to the Court of Reclamations[14]. Here is what our heavenly advisors taught us:

What has been stolen from you?

That you could ask Holy Spirit, "Where have I been stolen from?" Heaven is in a good mood to give back what has been taken from the saints. Often, you have been stolen from due to broken walls which correlate to bloodline iniquities, but having worked through the bloodline iniquities, now you can engage Heaven regarding theft from your realm, your destiny.[15]

---

[14] This chapter taken from my book, *Engaging Angels in the Realms of Heaven* (LifeSpring Publishing (2020)).

[15] I do not want to imply that simply by going through this book that everything is done. You may have other work to do concerning generational cleansing. This book is a vital step and reclaiming what was

Where do you feel you have been stolen from? When YOU have been stolen from, Satan also stole from the Kingdom of Heaven. You need to regain a certain degree of outrage at the enemy at being stolen from, with the understanding that what you are perceiving is the enemy has thieved from the Kingdom itself. It gives Heaven great pleasure to return to the saints what has been stolen.

Stolen from Previous Generations

This even includes what has been stolen in previous generations. Many saints do not come to ask for what has been stolen from your ancestry thinking only of the current generation or your current life; but Yahweh is always in a mood to release what has been stolen from previous generations. Appear in the Courts of Heaven to ask what can be reclaimed in the Court of Reclamation. Do not just appear there once but keep coming back. This Court of Reclamation is one that gives both counsel and adjudication regarding many losses perceived by a great many generations.

However, one trip to the Court of Reclamations is not a carte blanc arrangement where you can request everything ever lost to the enemy to be returned to you. It is vital that you listen to the counsel of Heaven and request only what the court recommends you petition for. You will be allowed to return over and over as needed. If you were to get back all that has ever been stolen from your or your generations all at once, you would be like the many lottery winners who are rich in a day and broke in two or three

---

lost to the enemy is vitally important for you. Please continue the work of cleansing.

years because they did not know how to handle the riches that came their way. We must learn to be stewards over that which is placed in our hands. Be patient with Heaven. Heaven wants you to have it all restored, but also trust the wisdom of Heaven in the process of restoration.

Be the One!

Be the one in your bloodline to begin the restoration of all things. You will have great pleasure in doing this. Many live in lack because of the condition of generational lack. Be the one in your bloodline to reverse the curse, utilizing the Court of Reclamation, to bring adjudication for your bloodline of many things that are still impacting it. This is not just wealth. This is creative flow, salvations, new books, and new scrolls. Anything that was blocked by iniquity or sin. As an individual's bloodline is cleansed and purified by the blood of Jesus, you can have hope in the ability to stand righteously in the Reclamation Court to receive an unlocking of what was blocked.

Many things have been blocked by current events, so go to the courts and avail yourself of the Court of Reclamation. Let it not be said in Heaven that we did not come to ask. This is the joy for which the Lord died upon the cross.

Get it ALL Back!

There is a way to get it all back, but many have not done so from the court level. You have attempted to through petitions and supplications, but you have not appeared in court.

Did you ask the counsel of the court?

What might you ask for from the Court – whether large or small?

Here is a hint. Remember that you do not know all things, therefore, how could you possibly know what to ask for in that court at times? Wait upon the counsel of the Holy Spirit and request the counsel of the court, as all things are done in perfect timing.

Because of the goodness and grace of God and what is coming, if you do not appear there in the Court of Reclamation to begin the process, you can never receive what is meant to come back to you.

Are we desensitized to loss?

We have become desensitized to loss. The theft of Satan has existed for so long on the earth that humanity has put up with it and, in some measure, accepted your loss. This was <u>never</u> the plan of the Father. We have no idea how timely this understanding is.

Ask the Holy Spirit to give you the grace NOT to be desensitized to the loss when you have access to the courts to make the enemy pay back.

In your future:

- I see piles of gold.
- I see piles of herbs and plants and growing things.
- I see piles of transportation-oriented things.
- I see piles of calendars and clocks and stopwatches.
- I see piles of what can be described as fountains.
- I see butterfly nets and fishing nets and harvesting nets.

These are the things waiting to be claimed through the court work.

Chapter 13
Plundering the Enemies Camp

As you recover using the Court of Reclamation[16] what has been lost to the enemy, Heaven has another option for restoration for God's sons and daughters. Taken from my book, *Engaging Angels in the Realms of Heaven*, this instruction is both helpful and encouraging. Here is what Heaven had to say:

"Provision is being released, but the provision trains[17] need protection. This provision is from the Father's storehouses. The delivery of provision has a timing component to it as well, so the delivery and timing needs to be protected as well."

> *We do charge and commission our angel(s) and their ranks to protect the provision that is coming to us. Protect it on its way. See that what has been slated for release comes to manifestation.*

"Are there weapons that you need for that?" we asked.

---

[16] This chapter taken from my book, *Engaging Angels in the Realms of Heaven* (LifeSpring Publishing (2020)).
[17] The trains that carry the provision.

In our situation we knew he had maps, but he requested something called guideposts. These are recognized by angels. On earth we have traffic signals on thoroughfares. Angels have guideposts and know the markings of the guideposts. We made the request of the Father and Heaven continued in our instruction.

Heaven told us that we need to begin to think in terms of offense, not defense, regarding the provision that the Father has for us. Ezekiel was suggesting an offensive stance. He explained, "There is provision that comes based on your giving, your offerings, and your obedience where you see the field that is yours – the ministry's field, where you know you have harvest. It is good to make sure it is protected."

Defense would be where we go to the Court of Reclamation and get back what the enemy has stolen, but offensive measures are about the provision *that is being released*. This comes from the faith that you have that you will be receiving the provision and you are expecting provision. You have done things like make withdrawals from the Finance Department for it, sown in obedience, and requested the provision. It is an offensive stance of protection over the coming prosperity, the release of windfalls, and things like that. We need to learn how to protect it offensively.

Rain from Heaven

We asked Lydia (our Business Advisor from the realms of Heaven) to help us understand.

She began, "It is not as hard as you think. Think of provision as rain from Heaven. The rain is coming, and you must put out your pots to receive it. What happens between the time it leaves the clouds and ends up in the pot? It is that period that needs protecting.

So, we need to charge our angel(s) and their ranks to offensively and aggressively war against the theft or potential theft, derailment, or capture by rerouting of the rain of provision that has been released from the Father to the ministry. This would look like a commissioning of our angels to do this. Ezekiel[18] has maps that he uses for this, as he instructs his ranks to an offensive position, not just defensive.

It is the difference between telling the ranks of angels to protect, but you can also tell them to plunder.

The Heavenly host is not looking for a fight from the enemy because they know whose they are and they know the fight is already won, but when the fight comes to them and the enemy makes an attack, you have traditionally stationed your angels to defend what is yours, but...

Now release them also to not only defend what is yours, but to plunder the enemy's camp.

Wouldn't you want that? To plunder is to make Satan pay when he brings the fight, and he loses.

---

[18] Ezekiel is the Chief Angel over our ministry. We engage him regularly for wisdom and input.

Always make the enemy pay by plundering the enemy's camp.

Do not think of camp as singular, *think of the many camps of the enemy from which he attacks you, the staff, the clients, the communication lines, and the provision.* Release your angels to war *defensively*, but **also** *offensively* to plunder the enemy's camp and gain back what belongs to the Kingdom of God. This would be a warfare activity that Ezekiel is well equipped for. At that point, Ezekiel was demonstrating his agreement with this and his 'can't wait' attitude.

Now Lydia showed a sack of gold and said all the gold and all the silver is the Father's (Haggai 2:8). "The enemy has for eons collected the gold through various means and by various ways, but now is the time to release your angels to plunder the enemy's camps and get back the gold," she explained.

Do you see there is a difference here in the reclamation court where you go for legal means? You can also release angelic activity to plunder the enemy's camp. So, where the enemy has stolen from people who do not even know how to get it back,

---
Heaven is saying the gold can be retrieved by any who will.

To get the portion of it back is the Father's goal, but if you get it back, it is credited to your action – the action of releasing the angels to the task - in some measure, **no matter who forfeited it.** It is still God's gold. Someone has just got to retrieve it. This falls to the mature saints of God who understand the ways of Yahweh and who are already operating in obedience as true sons.

We asked to be coached in this process and we were told:

It is like a commissioning in which we charge Ezekiel and his ranks so we can capture from the enemy that which has been stolen. Heaven wants to restore to us things that have been stolen – not only from us, but from those that we minister to, from those are associated with the ministry, their families, from their future (or from their past). In every arena, we are plundering to recover all that has been stolen in Jesus' name.

"When the angels recover the bounty, what is the distribution of that?" we asked.

It comes back to the one who requests it. See your angels as mighty warriors.

> *Your angels can get what is yours, but they can also get whatever is available.*

If you plunder an enemy camp and you see an object that he took from someone you know, you can say, "I am going to go get that. I see where the enemy took this whole room full of treasure from the kingdom of God, so I claim that too." That is the plundering of the enemy's camp.

We do not really need to understand or see the distribution. We will just experience it. We will just do this and see what happens.

How to speak to your angel(s):

> *"We commission you to go to your defensive stance in protection of the provision coming to the ministry, and we also commission you to your offensive stance as well for you*

and your ranks. We commission you to offensively plunder the enemy's camp, gain what has been stolen and return it to where it needs to go, in Jesus' name."

If you are a Kingdom citizen and the Kingdom has been plundered, you are able to loose angelic hosts to get back whatever the Kingdom lost, whether it is yours or not. This is your right. You have a right to that, but you are also operating as an ambassador of the Kingdom to get back what belongs to the Kingdom and let the King determine what he will do with it. Heaven just wants it back, but Heaven needs sons who will stand in their place and see to it that the plundering of the enemy's camp occurs. Saints – take your place!

Chapter 14
Conclusion

Are you finished? Not necessarily. The process of cleansing our bloodlines is exactly that – a process. It is not over simply because we read a book or prayed some prayers. However, the effort expended in working through this book took some diligence and commitment. I congratulate you on completing the process. You may find that, in the future, Holy Spirit will have you pick up this book again and go back through the courtroom scenarios. Maybe you will not have to for all the degree levels. It may be that some degree levels had more personal impact than others. Do not be discouraged. The freedom for you and your generations is worth all the effort.

Pray in the Spirit

If you pray in the spirit that would be a good way to tune your spirit to the realms of Heaven. It will provide a stirring within your spirit that will help you as you readjust to your life post-Mithraism influences.

Learn to Possess Your Realm

It is a learning process to possess your realm. You are a realm and yet an individual is made up of many realms. The spirit of a person is a realm, their soul is a realm, their body is another realm. Their family constitutes a realm. A person's business or employment is a realm. Within these realms are territories.

Learning to possess your realm means learning what is in your realm that needs to go and learning what needs to come in. It is learning how it needs to be filled, how it needs to stay filled, and how angels help with that and work with that. It is also learning how to invite the characteristics and qualities of the Father into your realm. You want the fruit of the spirit in your realm. You experience that by yielding your realm and the territories of your realm to that working of the Holy Spirit.

You have different parts of your overall realm that are more associated with your humanity. For example, your soul is a realm within your overall realm. Your soul helps define your personality, your emotions, intellect, and more. When you think in terms of realms, you begin to ascertain their ability to change and all of this relies on your desire, your intention, and your choice.

The understanding of realms and how to possess them and give your angels charge to guard your realms are some of the things that the enemy has known for a long time and he used evil people to shut down. If he could not shut that understanding down in a person, he would steal it. He would steal their realm by filling it with himself. You read in the previous chapter about commissioning your angel(s) to plunder but you need to do more than that. You need to commission them to guard your realms, gates[19], and bridges[20]. (I discuss this in my book *Engaging Angels in the Realms of Heaven*). Simply call your angel near and say something similar to this:

> *I call my angel near and I commission you to guard my realms, gates, and bridges. Allow in only what is written in my scroll and remove anything within my realms, gates, or bridges that are not part of the Father's destiny for my life, I also charge you to cleanse my realms of all spiritual debris from the court work that has been done regarding Mithraism. I charge you to this in Jesus' name.*

Invite Jesus Into Your Realm

Those who are in the son, in Jesus, their first thing is to invite him into their realm. You have known this in a lens or perspective called salvation, and the effect is somewhat similar. You are inviting the living God in representation of Himself as His son Jesus to take up residence in your realm. Simply invite Jesus into your overall realm by the words of your mouth. In all these instructions be sure to speak aloud the commissions and invitations. It is necessary for activation.

---

[19] Gates are access points to your realm. Your eyes and ears are access points among many others.

[20] Bridges are the pathways to other realms as in relationships.

Call Your Spirit Forward

You will want to call your spirit forward and instruct it to help your soul adjust and mend from the influences it has been under.

Practice Your Spiritual Seeing

Often one's spiritual sight has been affected by the oaths and covenants taken in Mithraism and you will need to begin to practice seeing with your spirit eyes now that the veils have been removed. (See my book *Unlocking Spiritual Seeing* for more tips on this subject.)

Journal

Dr. Mark Virkler has written extensively on this subject over the years. It is his signature teaching, and he has helped thousands of believers learn to hear and record what Heaven is saying to them on an ongoing basis. His website[21] has a myriad of materials to assist you in learning to do spirit-led journaling. I will simply summarize his teaching here because it is a vital discipline for you to learn to maximize Heaven down in your life.

1. **Quiet yourself** – Learn to quiet yourself so you can tune into Heaven.
2. **Look unto Jesus** – we are not looking for anyone outside of Heaven to be speaking to us—they are not invited to the party!

---

[21] www.cwgministries.org (Communion with God Ministries)

3. **Tune to the Flow of the Spirit Within** – The Holy Spirit flows through our spirit like a river. We can learn to tune to that flow and hear what Heaven is saying.
4. **Write it down!** —Begin to record what you are hearing or perceiving. YOU can judge it when you are finished listening for Heaven. Do not concern yourself with how it looks on the page. Just record it—whether handwritten, drawn, or typed, make a record of it![22]

Deal with the Freemasonry in Your Lineage

The other insidious false religion that affects a large portion of people on the planet in Freemasonry. If you are of European descent, you likely have Freemasonry in your background. If you are black descent and your ancestors were slaves, the likelihood is strong that slave owners were Freemasons and therefore your lineage has been impacted. If you are of Hispanic descent, then you will likely need to deal with Aztec, Incan, or Myan issues. If of oriental descent, then those cultures typically had their version of Freemasonry. Other cultures had various versions but it all boils down to profane worship of other gods and we all need to be free.

My book *Overcoming the False Verdicts of Freemasonry* will help you get free of Freemasonry in your life and lineage. You may have prayed prayers of renunciation, but my book goes deeper than simply renouncing Freemasonry. It helps you deal with the false verdicts that empower every degree level of Freemasonry so you can truly be free. It is crafted similarly to this book and has

---

[22] At CourtsNet.com you will find our video course to help you in this process.

helped hundreds, if not thousands gain new levels of freedom in their life.

Learn the Power of Spiritual Bonds

In my book *Releasing Bonds from the Courts of Heaven* I discuss the power of spiritual bonds. A little-known aspect to the Bride of Christ are the power godly bonds can have upon your life. My book will teach you how to get them working in your life. You will also learn how to get ungodly bonds removed from your life. Ungodly bonds are not unlike chains that keep something in place in your life. Learn how to deal with them so you can live free as Heaven has designed for you to live.

It is our prayer for you that you experience freedom on levels never experienced before. We request for you bonds[23] of absolute freedom from every bondage, bonds of peace, and bonds of hope, in Jesus' name.

As you go forward, you will experience a lightness and freedom you have never felt before. Your soul will be reacclimating to the new atmosphere in your life now that you have dealt with the vestiges of Mithraism and their impact on your life. Send us your testimonies of freedom and the impact his has had on your life. We would love to hear from you.

Blessings to you of hope, revelation, freedom, and great joy, in Jesus' name.

---

[23] To learn about spiritual bonds, see my book *Releasing Bonds from the Courts of Heaven*.

Works Cited

Crabtree, V. (2017). *Mithraism and Early Christianity*. Retrieved from Mithraism and Early Christianity: http://www.vexen.co.uk/religion/mithraism.html

Appendix A

A Short Explanation of Lingering Human Spirits

Recently someone asked me about this subject as they had been told I had said something I did not say. I try to be incredibly careful with what I say and some words I simply do not use to minimize the confusion. However, just like the children's game where one person whispers something in the ear of the person beside them, and that person does the same to the person beside them until it goes around the entire room — invariably, what is heard by the last person was nowhere close to what had been originally said. The following is a brief explanation about LHS's[24] that you might find useful. This is what I wrote:

I thought I would try to clear up your concerns about what I refer to as lingering human spirits that we dealt with in your session. The verse[25] you mentioned is not doctrine and does not include or exclude a time frame in-between the two events — dying and judgment. Nor

---

[24] LHS = Lingering Human Spirit
[25] Hebrews 9:27 And as it is appointed for men to die once, but after this the judgment.

is the verse to be absent from the body is to be present from the Lord[26] — that was Paul's anticipation. As a believer they can expect to move immediately into Heaven, but not all who die are ready to begin eternity and are hesitant to begin, therefore the spirit wanders around seeking rest or a resting place. The unbelieving spirit certainly does not want to step into their eternity and will do everything in their power to remain, even if it involves wandering in the waterless place. Those who die in battle may be resolved to die but are usually hoping to not die. Those whose death is by murder or genocide were not desiring to die, but it was forced upon their bodies. These spirits wander seeking rest as Jesus spoke of in Matthew 12:43-45 (also in Luke 11). Understand that the use of the word "unclean spirit" was to differentiate between them and the Holy Spirit. It also was a reference to the spirit being ceremonially unclean based on Jewish tradition. The Jews had an entire process for preparation for burial (remember the death of Jesus and the women that brought spices to prepare Jesus' body for burial).

The Matthew 12 passage of scripture was poorly translated which is partially why we always thought it was talking about demons. Unclean spirits are not demons. Revelation 18:3 points this out as well. There is more to be said but this should summarize it for you. To have a lingering human spirit is not typically some evil thing; they were simply looking for a body to live out their destiny in and since their body was no longer available, they hitched a ride with you. That is especially common when babies die — they do not want to leave mama. Releasing them to Heaven is a simple thing as you experienced the other day. They have a destiny in Heaven too! We will just help them begin it.

---

[26] 2 Corinthians 5:8

Once an LHS is discerned, simply call them to come forward so you can assist them to make their transition into their eternity. Our heavenly Father desires to populate Heaven, not hell. Speak to the LHS and advise them that it is time for them to step into their eternity. Remind them that they can call upon the mercy of the Lord when they stand before Him. Invite angels to assist them in this process. Then, open the silver channel[27] allowing them to enter Heaven to stand before the Father.

Once they have transitioned, close the silver channel by saying, "I now close the silver channel, in Jesus' name." You have now helped these wandering spirits to begin their destiny in Heaven.

For a fuller explanation, see my book, Lingering Human Spirits available in paperback, PDF, and Kindle:

www.courtsofheaven.net/store

---

[27] The silver channel is a portal for spirits to transition from where they are into eternity.

A Testimony

A testimony from one of our students after they had gone through the courtroom scenarios developed for this book for freedom from Mithraism.

Upon going back into the Fourth Degree, again, I invited in the bloodlines. When the 4th verdict came, this time something vastly different happened than all other times. Jesus came forward walking through the center of the court, we were all then given elements for communion. I could see the nail marks in his hands and feet as he walked past me, even his pierced side. Everyone in the court in our bloodlines participated in communion, we all worshipped Jesus and then started singing "come all ye faithful". I felt like I needed to go take communion now in the natural. After this I went upstairs to take communion in to celebrate the freedom. As a testimony to see this was really manifesting in the earth, I needed to include the following:

As I walked upstairs after about 2 hours of doing these repentances my 10-year-old stepson (who is usually not one for wanting to willingly participate in church or reading the bible, etc.) comes running over and says, can we take communion. Then my other stepson and 3-year-old also say yes let us do "Kiddush" (Hebrew blessings before taking the wine). I was just bowled over with amazement for how the Lord is setting these kids free. We took communion together. My stepson even wanted to lead explaining the importance of the Matzah and Grape juice as being the blood and body of Christ and I explained to them the importance of the covenant Jesus made. This to me and my wife is nothing short of miraculous, praise God!

-JF

Description

The Body of Christ is being awakened to the extent to which paganism has been intertwined with Christianity throughout the centuries. Many traditions and teachings that we accept as part of Christianity have, upon closer examination, been borrowed from ancient pagan religions. These spiritual connections to pagan entities are creating unnecessary bondages in the Body of Christ.

The false religion of Mithraism has been a major factor in the world, but its role has been kept largely hidden. *Freedom from Mithraism* will help you cancel the false verdicts that are impacting your life and your generations because of this pagan religion and will move you into new places of freedom. Most religious movements have been impacted by Mithraism. It is time to get free!

About the Author

Dr. Ron Horner is a communicator and best-selling author of twenty books on the subjects of the Courts of Heaven and engaging the realms of Heaven. He teaches through weekly classes, training programs, seminars, and conferences.

Ron is the founder of LifeSpring International Ministries, which serves to advocate for both individuals and businesses in the Courts of Heaven. He is also the founder of Business Advocate Services, a worldwide consulting company (BASGlobal.net).

Other Books by Dr. Ron M. Horner

Building Your Business from Heaven Down

Building Your Business from Heaven Down 2.0

Cooperating with The Glory

Engaging Angels in the Realms of Heaven

Engaging Heaven for Revelation – Volume 1

Engaging the Courts for Ownership & Order

Engaging the Courts for Your City (Paperback, Leader's Guide & Workbook)

Engaging the Courts of Healing & the Healing Garden

Engaging the Courts of Heaven

Engaging the Help Desk of the Courts of Heaven

Engaging the Mercy Court of Heaven

Four Keys to Dismantling Accusations

Let's Get it Right!

Lingering Human Spirits

Overcoming the False Verdicts of Freemasonry

Overcoming Verdicts from the Courts of Hell

Releasing Bonds from the Courts of Heaven

The Courts of Heaven Process Charts

Unlocking Spiritual Seeing

www.ingramcontent.com/pod-product-compliance
Lightning Source LLC
Chambersburg PA
CBHW051806040426
42446CB00007B/550